BEING CHURCH 101

MARK HEARN

CROSS
BOOKS

CrossBooks™
1663 Liberty Drive
Bloomington, IN 47403
www.crossbooks.com
Phone: 1-866-879-0502

First published by CrossBooks 6/10/2009

ISBN: 978-1-6150-7031-2 (sc)

All scriptures are HCSB unless otherwise noted.

Printed in the United States of America
Bloomington, Indiana

This book is printed on acid-free paper.

Dedicated to the wonderful people of the churches whom I have been privileged to serve as senior pastor for these past twenty-eight years.

Brown Springs Baptist Church, Mosheim, Tennessee

Payneville Baptist Church, Payneville, Kentucky

Hillcrest Baptist Church, Morristown, Tennessee

First Baptist Church, Seymour, Tennessee

Grace Baptist Church, Evansville, Indiana

Calvary Baptist Temple, Savannah, Georgia

Northside Baptist Church, Indianapolis, Indiana

With special thanks to Denni Bannister for taking on the monumental task of typing this manuscript. May God bless you and your family!

CONTENTS

FOREWORD

The year was 1983. I was a new seminary student at the Southern Baptist Theological Seminary in Louisville, Kentucky. Because the seminary at that time was more leftward leaning, a group of conservative students formed an alliance of sorts. We called ourselves "the roundtable," because we often gathered at a large round table in the student center.

I may have been the least theologically savvy at that table. Unlike most of my peers, my undergraduate training was in finance, and I had been a banker vocationally for several years before I responded to God's call to ministry.

But in 1983 I was clueless. I needed help. I needed a mentor and a friend.

And I found both in Mark Hearn.

I was drawn to Mark for several reasons. For one, he had great abilities that were only exceeded by a great humility. He was clearly the best preacher among us. I could have listened to his sermons all day long. Indeed, I often used Mark as a point of reference of good preaching to compare to my pathetic oratory skills.

Mark seemed to have that old fashioned common sense that many pastors just don't seem to have. I could go to Mark for counsel, and his words were so on target that I was often embarrassed that I didn't see things as clearly as he did. Indeed as Mark has served churches across the United States, it seems that God has placed him into positions that call for extraordinary wisdom and good old common sense.

Mark Hearn is a leader in churches. He has and is serving in so many places of leadership in our denomination that I sometimes lose count.

So why I am telling you all these things about Mark? Quite simply, I think of few people who are so gifted to tell the story of Being Church 101. Mark has the background. He has the gifts and skills. He has the training. And above all, he has the heart. He simply loves the local church.

But Mark Hearn would be the first to tell you that his background, gifts, skills, and accomplishments are insufficient to tell the story of the local church. He instead uses all those gifts to turn to the Word of God. This is an amazing book about an amazing church, the church at Corinth. Now, to say that the Corinthian church is an amazing church is not to say the church had no problems. Quite the contrary.

But Mark Hearn takes all the woes of the church in 1 Corinthians to show us how we can be the Church today. His exposition is compelling. His story telling is fascinating. And God's truth is pervasive in this book.

You, the reader, are in for a treat. Read what one of the great expositors of today says the Bible says about the local church. Mark Hearn pulls no punches. You will come away from a reading of Being the Church 101 better instructed, better motivated, and better prepared.

I am glad I met Mark Hearn in 1983. I am glad to still call him friend today.

And, if you don't know him, you will be glad you met him through this book.

Get ready for an amazing journey in Scripture.

And enjoy the travels as you learn about Being the Church 101.

Thom S. Rainer
President and CEO LifeWay Christian Resources

INTRODUCTION

The title of this book is *Being Church 101*. That may sound a little unusual, but it is rooted in Paul's advice to the Church at Corinth and his instructions to the people to be the church. "Being church" is not a phrase we usually hear. Some people merely play church. Remember in your childhood days how you played school or house. Maybe you even played church where someone sat in a pew and someone got to be the song leader and someone was the preacher. For some it is still a game. They ask, "How fast can I get there and how fast can I get home?" I remember a comment from one chairman of the ushers in a church I once attended. "Pastor, can we open up the doors during the closing prayer? People are going to hurt themselves trying to get out of here," he said.

For some people, church life is all about the game. Since the 1930s, Gallup has asked Americans in its annual poll, "Do you attend church regularly?" The consistent result has shown that about 40 percent of Americans attend church regularly. Now attendance goes up a little bit at times and down a little bit at times, but remarkably, it has remained at this level for more than seven decades. But the survey also has found that today only about 20 percent of Americans actually attend church even though 40 percent say that they attend regularly. So Gallup's researchers decided that they would come up with some follow-up questions, including, "What do you consider to be regular church attendance?" People offered some interesting answers to that one. "Well, I usually go," or "Weddings and funerals I'm there." Some even counted church picnics and carnivals on the church parking lot.[1] You might say that these people are just playing church. For them, attending church is just about having a good time.

Other people avoid church. Did you realize that 60 percent of regular church attendees become church dropouts during their years between high school and twenty-one years of age? It is interesting that among these young American adults, 80 percent says religious faith is "very important."[2] So 80 percent says religious faith is very important, but six in ten of them have dropped out of the church. What does that say for the church?

Thom Rainer, president of LifeWay Christian Resources, has co-written a book with his son, Sam Rainer, entitled *Essential Church*. In that book, the Rainers point out that we have a generation in which the majority is avoiding church. We need, therefore, to exemplify how essential the church is to the body of Christ.

Some people are playing church, some people are avoiding church, and some people are "doing church." For the vast majority of people who regularly attend church, church is something they "do." Think about how you use the word "church" in your everyday conversation. Some talk about "going to church." Some talk about "giving to the church." Some talk about "serving the church." For the vast majority of people, church points to activities they "do."

Paul's advice to the Corinthians is not about "playing church," not about "avoiding church," and not even about "doing church." Instead, he advises the Corinthians to start "being the church." Now, I'm not interested in resolutions about how often you attend church. That may come as a surprise to many of you. Recently I was doing some research online and found the Web site *www.mygoals.com*. You might want to look this up. This Web site has been tracking New Year's resolutions for the past several years. Its online survey reports the top resolutions in 2009 involved "health & fitness." Twenty-three percent of individuals surveyed made a health or fitness resolution this year. The top health and fitness resolution was to lose weight. Also among the top resolutions was "personal finance." The number-one resolution in the area of personal finance was to pay down credit cards. Fourteen percent made resolutions in this area. Thirteen percent made resolutions involving "personal growth and interest." The leading resolutions in that area were to "read a book" or to "learn a new language." Eight percent made resolutions in the area of "education and training" to complete a degree. Eight percent made resolutions in "family and relationships." This category doubled over the previous year. The number-one response in this category was to "spend more time with my family." Eight percent made resolutions relating to "home improvement." Many said, "I'm not moving in the midst of this economy, so I'd better fix up what I have."

As I read through this list, questions kept coming to mind: "What about God? Where is God in this survey? Where are 'spiritual' thoughts in this survey?" After reading through page upon page of this survey, I found that the issues of spirituality appeared among the responses of the 13 percent who said that they made resolutions in areas of "personal growth and interest." And of those, less than 2 percent made a spiritual goal for 2009![3]

Most likely, few people have set spiritual goals for this year. But I'm suggesting a goal for each of you to embrace. I want you to join me in embracing a life that says, "I'm with you in being the church." That's the same goal that Paul gave to the Corinthians: "Be the church."

LESSON 1
CHURCHES HAVE PROBLEMS

How did Paul advise the Corinthians to "Be the church"? Lesson number one about being the church is to realize that churches have problems. Now, some of you already are checking out and saying, "Duh!" It helps to realize a number of people enter into church and don't know that churches have problems. An example is the lady who visited a church and inquired about its ministries, telling the pastor, "I visited a hundred churches. I'm in search of the perfect church." The pastor said, "When you find it, don't join it. It won't be perfect anymore." Churches have problems; it doesn't take long when reading 1 Corinthians to know that the Corinthian church had all kinds of problems. This letter from Paul has been called the "handbook of church difficulties." Some of the themes that we'll cover as we go through 1 Corinthians include: church divisions; litigation between church members; deterioration of the family unit; disorderly worship services; moral failures; adultery; homosexuality; doctrinal differences; and tight-fisted Christians who aren't willing to give to the church. It amazes me that there are literally dozens of churches named "Corinth Church." Have they read 1 Corinthians?

It all began with a little church in a metropolitan city called Corinth, one of the leading economic centers of the entire Roman Empire. A city of about half a million people, it was most noted for its immorality. It was famous as the home of the Temple of Aphrodite, the goddess of love. It was lax morally—so much so that references to the city were common in the vernacular of the day. To "Corinthianize"

1

meant to engage in sexually immoral behavior. Archaeological digs in Palestine have discovered an ancient slogan referring to the city: "What happens in Corinth stays in Corinth." You get the idea. It was that kind of city. On Paul's second missionary journey, he said, "What better place to establish a church than in the city of Corinth?" So in Corinth grew a church that Paul loved, that he remembered in prayer, and that confronted him with extensive problems.

Corinth Was a Defiled Church

In the first chapter of his letter, Paul alluded to three problems facing the church in Corinth. The first problem was that members were guilty of sexual immorality, drunkenness, and worldly living. Corinth was a city covered in filth; the church, in turn, reflected its city. The church comprised four factions competing for leadership and tearing at one another. It was a disgraceful church that had become a disgrace to the name of God, rather than glorifying him.

So how does one handle such serious church difficulties when they come into the life of a fellowship? In 1 Corinthians 1:1, Paul began his letter, noting that he was "an apostle of Jesus Christ." There were two types of apostles in the first century. The first included the original apostles, whom we call the disciples. They were the eyewitnesses of Jesus and his ministry. The second type included apostles appointed by the whole church. We probably would call them bishops or pastors. Paul wanted to be very clear that although he was not an eyewitness of Jesus' earthly ministry, he was a witness who had encountered the risen Christ. Thus he spoke and wrote, not with the authority of the church, but with the authority of Christ as "Paul, an apostle of Jesus Christ."

Paul did not mention defilement explicitly in 1 Corinthians 1. Even so, we'll find this theme appearing throughout the letter. Here, though, he began his letter by telling the church what its members ought to "be."

First, Christians ought to **be extraordinary.** Paul uses three words to describe the fellowship: church, sanctified, and saints. The word "church" was a very common word in Paul's day. It meant to be "called out," to be part of a gathering. There were varieties of gatherings in the first century. Any gathering of people around one central theme resulted, technically, in a "church." For example, people in Indianapolis, Indiana, where I serve as a pastor, will often have gatherings around their favorite theme, the Indianapolis Colts, our NFL franchise. Some might even admit that those gatherings make up their religion.

The second word Paul used to describe the early believers was "sanctified." The word "sanctified" means to be set apart or to be different. It points to a different kind of gathering, one separated from the world. And then the third word is "saints." Now saints are not dead people. Saints are living people. Adrian Rogers used to say, "We have a problem accepting our sainthood." There are only two kinds of people in this world, "saints" and "ain'ts."[1] Some are "saints" and some "ain't saints." You are a saint if you've given your life to Jesus Christ. A saint is someone who has been set apart by his or her relationship with Jesus Christ. So Paul addressed this letter to a gathering of people who were different from the world. What made them different from the world was that they had been set apart for Jesus Christ. This reminds me of a deacon in a church I had served who was a professional photographer. He told me about an occasion in which he was taking photographs at a wedding. He had positioned himself in the center aisle as the couple walked out. He was taking photographs in rapid succession, just one right after another. You know how wedding photographers work, taking what seemed like 50 photographs for every step the bride and groom take as they go down the aisle. When the couple reached the back of the auditorium, the groom peeled off to the side and the bride just kept going. She walked out the door, down the steps, into a waiting car with her ex-boyfriend. The photographer said it was the most unusual situation he had ever experienced. The people gathered inside didn't know what to do. And yet, there are people who do that every week, who claim to be part of the bride of Jesus Christ (his church) and walk out on it, wedding themselves to the world throughout the week. Paul said, "Be extraordinary. Be different!"

The second word from Paul was to **be enriched**: "I'll always thank my God for you because of God's grace given to you in Christ Jesus" (1 Cor. 1:4). In 1 Corinthians 1:7, Paul wrote, "so that you do not lack any spiritual gift as you eagerly wait." The word *grace* is the word *charis* in Greek. The word translated as *gift* is *charis-mata*, grace gift. It's where we get our word *charismatic.* Some of my charismatic friends may ask me, "Are you a charismatic?" I say, "Absolutely!" Charismatic means, "grace gift." I have received a gift by the grace of God. In 1 Corinthians 1:5, Paul wrote, "that by Him you were made rich in everything—in all speaking and in all knowledge." The word appearing as "made rich" or "enriched" in some translations comes from a compound Greek word, *pluto-crat.* It means to be extremely wealthy. I have been made extremely wealthy, not in physical wealth but in spiritual wealth by the grace which God has given me. And in 1 Corinthians 1:7, Paul wrote, "As the testimony about Christ was confirmed among you." I was made extremely wealthy spiritually when God confirmed his grace in my life. And when grace became confirmed in my life, I realized how extremely wealthy I was.

Slave trader John Newton came to know God's grace when he penned these words, "Amazing grace! How sweet the sound that saved a wretch like me. I once was lost, but now am found. Was blind, but now I see." Be extraordinary and be enriched.

The third thing Paul told the church was to **be expectant**. He wrote, "As you eagerly wait for the revelation of our Lord Jesus Christ" (1 Cor. 1:7). You know the best way to stay pure? The best way to deal with defilement is to expect that the Lord could come back at any time. It could happen today. As Paul wrote, "He will also confirm you to the end, blameless in the day of our Lord Jesus Christ" (1 Cor.1:8). Because I am blameless, I am looking forward to the day in which Jesus returns. Please be very careful to note that Paul did not say *guiltless.* He said *blameless.* None of us is guiltless. But if we are forgiven, we are blameless. No accusations can be brought against us, because someone has already forgiven us. I can be expectant and look forward to God coming in Jesus Christ, because I have been forgiven. Paul dealt with the defiled church by telling them to "live holy."

Corinth Was a Divided Church

Division was the second problem facing this church. Division has a long history as a problem among God's people. It has been so since the dawn of humanity. Almost all New Testament writings have some portion dealing with the problem of division in the church. "To live above with saints we love, oh that will be glory. But to live below with saints we know, oh now that's another story."

The Corinthians needed to learn how to get along with one another. Paul instructed this divided church, listing three corrective measures for its members. First of all, they needed to understand **the correct person**: "Now I urge you, brothers, in the name of our Lord Jesus Christ, that you all say the same thing, and that there be no divisions among you" (1 Cor. 1:10). The word *division* is the translation of *schismata*. It is the word that means "crack" or "split." The problem in Corinth was that they emphasized the messenger rather than the message. Thus they were divided. According to 1 Corinthians 1:12, "Some say that you are of Paul," the founder of the church. In effect, the congregation's charter members were remembering, "Oh, there was never anyone like brother Paul. He was the best. It's not been the same since brother Paul left here." Then Paul wrote, "Some of you are of Apollos" (1 Cor. 1:12). Acts 18:24 states, "Apollos, a man who is eloquent and mighty in the scriptures." There was no other Bible scholar like Apollos. Perhaps some members of the church in Corinth said, "Oh, have you ever heard someone preach like Apollos? He's probably the best preacher I've ever heard." Next Paul said, "Some of them say they are of Cephas," which is *Peter* in Aramaic (1 Cor. 1:12). There is no historical evidence that Peter ever visited the church at Corinth. But since Peter was an evangelist, even if he hadn't traveled to Corinth, he likely would have visited someplace where the Corinthians could have heard him preach. "Oh, if we would have just had someone with a burning passion like Cephas. He is just filled with passion." A fourth group of people said, "We're not getting into this personality squabble; we are of Christ. We are the true believers. We are the ones who will be here when everyone else leaves. We are the fellowship of the church."

This situation differs little from many of our church uprisings today, where some would say, "I am of Paul" or "I am of Apollos" or "I am of Cephas" or "I am of Christ." Paul declared they should become united. In 1 Corinthians 1:10, Paul wrote that the people ought to be perfectly joined or united together. This is the same thought that appears in Matthew's gospel when Jesus commanded the disciples to mend their nets. Paul meant, in effect, "If there's one word of advice I want to give you in the midst of your division, it is 'mend your nets,' because if there are holes in your nets, you are not going to be good fishermen. I am far more concerned with the catch. I'm far more concerned with the message than I am the messenger." Paul wrote in 1 Corinthians 1:13, "Would Christ be divided up?" The term is actually a very grotesque word that means "chopped up." Christ isn't chopped up. The body of Christ is still intact, in one piece. Our minds are chopped up; our allegiances are chopped up; our loyalties are chopped up. We need to seek unity in our evangelistic efforts.

Next Paul pointed the church to **the correct priority.** Paul said, "I'm not interested in bragging rights." I don't know of any pastor who has ever come back to a former ministry and made this statement: "I'm glad I didn't baptize any of you." Baptism is not the important thing. According to 1 Peter 3:21, "Baptism, which corresponds to this, now saves you (not the removal of the filth of the flesh, but the pledge of a good conscience towards God)." When Peter said baptism "now saves [us]," he explained parenthetically what he meant by that statement. Peter said that it was not the act of baptism itself, not the putting away the filth of the flesh, but the "answer of a good conscience towards God." The word "answer" was a word used when a judge officiated over the formation of a contract. A judge would ask in court, "Do you agree to the terms of this contract?" and the parties would answer, saying, "I do." Baptism saves us, not through the act of being dunked under water, but by the act of saying, "I do" to Jesus Christ. What is important? Paul said, "It's not whether I baptized any of you. The important thing is "have you answered God and said 'I do' to him?" 1 Corinthians 1:17 states, in effect, "I did not want to preach just with clever words like a Greek debater or like a used car salesman. But I wanted you to answer God with a sincere 'I do.'"

A divided church needs to worship the correct person, realize the correct priority, and also develop **the correct perspective.** Divided churches tend to debate the question, "What is the main thing?" The main thing is the cross. As 1 Corinthians 1:18-21 states, "For those who are perishing the message of the cross is foolishness, but to us who are being saved it is God's power. For it is written: 'I will destroy the wisdom of the wise, and I will set aside the understanding of the experts.' Where is the philosophy? Where is the scholar? Where is the debater of this age? Hasn't God made this world's wisdom foolish? For since in God's wisdom, the world didn't know God through wisdom, God was pleased to save those who believe through the foolishness of this message that's been preached." Paul said, "You wanted something that would unite us and get us together? Let's go back to the cross."

I realize that going back to the cross presents a choice of two perspectives: an unbeliever's perspective and a believer's perspective. Within the unbelieving perspective some adopt the Jewish unbelieving perspective. The Jewish unbeliever perspective says the cross is a "stumbling block." In Jewish law, someone who was crucified was considered to be accursed and it was absolutely impossible for a Jewish person to believe that their Messiah, their Savior, could go to the cross because he'd be accursed.

The second unbelieving perspective is that of a Greek. Among the Greeks, it was "foolishness," the translation of *moranos,* from which we get our words "moron" and "moronic." To some Greeks, it was just absolutely beyond human rationale that a dead Jewish Rabbi could be the Savior of the world. So among the unbelievers, it was a "Dumbo idea."

Among the believers, the preaching of the cross was "power!" The word *power* is the translation of *dunamis,* related to our word "dynamite." Paul said that if one wanted to bring together a divided people, then one took them to the cross where they had to make a decision. It is either a "Dumbo idea" or a "dynamo idea."

Corinth Was a Disgraced Church

Corinth had let far too much of its community affect the church rather than the church reaching out to affect the community. Paul said, "I want you to think about **your pilgrimage**." In 1 Corinthians 1:26, Paul wrote, "Brothers, consider your calling: not many are wise from the human perspective, not many powerful, not many of noble birth." I want you to look around and take inventory. There aren't many superstars among us. Now it doesn't say "not any"; it just says "not many." All of us know some superstars in Hollywood, sports, and business who are very outspoken about their faith. But, in reality, there aren't many. The ones who speak about faith certainly are not the majority. The Christian pilgrimage is made up of common ordinary people who follow the message about Jesus.

After he reminded them of his pilgrimage, Paul pointed out that there has always been **a plan**. 1 Corinthians 1:27-28 states, "Instead, God has chosen the world's foolish things to shame the wise, and God has chosen the world's weak things to shame the strong. God has chosen the world's insignificant and despised things—the things viewed as nothing—so that He might bring to nothing the things that are viewed as something." God's plan has always been to nullify anything that separates us from him, to render it worthless. God will certainly take care of or "bring to naught" (1 Cor. 1:28, KJV) anything that stands between him and us.

Paul also warned the Corinthians to consider in what they held the most **pride**. According to 1 Corinthians 1:30-31, "But from Him you are in Christ Jesus, who for us became wisdom from God, as well as righteousness, sanctification, and redemption, in order that, as is written: 'The one who boasts must boast in the Lord.'"

I don't know if you have a bragging problem, but when you do boast, what do you boast about? Well, you wouldn't brag about your paper airplane prowess if you were in the presence of a Boeing engineer. You wouldn't meet an aeronautical engineer and say, "Man, I can make the best paper airplane. I've actually sailed one thirty to forty yards." Likewise, you wouldn't brag about your putting ability if you were with Tiger Woods. "You know, Tiger, I sank a thirty-foot putt the other day." Tiger would yawn. Also, you wouldn't make a free throw shot in the presence of Michael Jordan and look over at Michael and say, "You know what? I got game! I'm the Man!"

So if you wouldn't brag about your paper airplane prowess before a Boeing engineer and you wouldn't brag about your putting ability to Tiger Woods and you wouldn't brag about your free throw shots in a conversation with Michael Jordan, then why in the world would you brag about your goodness if you are in the presence of a perfect, holy and almighty God? That's why Isaiah said, "All our righteousness is like a filthy rag" (Isa. 64:6). 1 Corinthians 1:31 actually presents a loose quotation of Jeremiah 9:24, "But the one who boasts should boast in this, that he understand and he knows Me—that I am the Lord and I am showing faithful love, justice, and righteousness on the earth, for I delight in these things. This is the Lord's declaration." The only thing that you have to boast about is to boast that God knows you and God loves you anyway! "Let him who boasts, boast in this. Let him boast in the Lord" (1 Cor. 1:31).

One of the most prolific hymn writers of all time was Fanny Crosby. She wrote:

> Redeemed, how I love to proclaim it.
> Redeemed by the blood of the Lamb.
> Redeemed through His infinite mercy,
> His child and forever I am.

That great blind hymn writer said, "Redeemed, how I love to proclaim it. Redeemed, how I love to tell people about it. Redeemed, how I love to share what Christ has done for me." If you are ready to make a decision, let that decision be not to play church, not to avoid church, or even to do church. Instead, decide to say, "Yes, Lord, we will 'be the church.' We will be the redeemed and people will know we are Christians by our love."

LESSON 2
GET ON THE SAME PAGE

How do you get the members of a large organization on the same page? No matter what kind of organization, whether it's a civic organization, a volunteer group, a business or a church, the question remains: how do you get that organization's members on the same page? I did some research online and came across a Web site, *www.BusinessKnowledgeSource.com*. It featured an article about five steps to unify your company. Here's something I can sink my teeth into: How do you get a company's employees on the same page? The experts say:

1. Provide Clear Goals—If you are the head of an organization, you need to be able to get everybody working towards the same goal. You cannot work together if not everyone knows where you are headed. But if you are all moving in the same direction, you increase productivity.

2. Choose people who will work well together—Identify individual strengths and use their strengths to maximize performance. When everyone contributes his or her best effort, the result is multiplied. Get people in the right place at the right time doing the right things.

3. Hire skilled people in the first place—Look for people who have natural abilities and who are also passionate about what they do, individuals who always give their best to the job.

4. Encourage motivation—Since most people are already somewhat motivated or they wouldn't be in the position or the job to begin with, create an atmosphere in which everyone encourages one another. Everyone then does his or her best and the organization thrives.

5. Balance work with life—People are happier and they perform better when their life is in proper balance, when they have proper priorities, when they hold the part of their life in proper perspective.[1]

Wonderful advice! Did Paul give any of these pointers to the Church at Corinth? The answers would be "No! Absolutely none of them." When he was called upon to bring the large organization of the church of Jesus Christ together in the city of Corinth, Paul didn't use one word of these supposed expert techniques.

Remember that Paul wrote 1 Corinthians in response to a letter from the congregation in which the people enumerated their problems. It must have caused Paul pain to realize that a church in which he had served like a midwife at its birth was filled with the three kinds of problems we explored in the last chapter. The church at Corinth was a defiled church; it was filled with impurities. The people had allowed the world to influence the church rather than working for the church to influence the world. The church at Corinth was divided, with factions competing for leadership. Finally, the church at Corinth was disgraced; its members had forgotten their purpose and were, therefore, just wandering aimlessly.

So where did Paul start in his efforts to correct the church? Where did he start in getting everybody on the same page? He started with doctrine. It is always amazing to me what some people consider to be a compliment on one of my sermons. I recall when one person said, "Pastor, that was the kind of sermon I like. There wasn't any doctrine in it or nothing." That is true to the core. If there is no doctrine in a sermon, it was probably nothing.

Where does encouragement come from? Where does unity come from unless by correct doctrine? Ephesians 4:2-6 states:

> ...with all humility and gentleness, with patience, accepting one another in love, diligently keeping the

unity of the Spirit with the peace that binds us. There's one body, one Spirit just as you recall the one hope of your calling; one Lord, one faith, one baptism, one God and Father of all, who is above all and through all and in all.

The Bible teaches repeatedly that unification takes place when we are correct in our patterns of thinking, that is, when we are correct in our doctrine. Paul was saying, in effect, "If you want to get on the same page, church of Corinth—you divided, defiled church and disgraced church—then get to a point of unity of doctrine."

Having received this letter from the Corinthians enumerating their difficulties, Paul basically said, "Before we discuss any of the specific problems that you have as a church, let's be sure that we are of one mind concerning this. Let's be sure that we are on the same page. Let's go back to the very tenets of our faith, the very fundamentals, to be sure that all of us are clicking on the same cylinders."

The Message is "Purchased By the Son"

We can find three fundamentals of the gospel message in 1 Corinthians 2. The first is that **the Son purchases us**. Paul started the chapter, writing, "When I came to you brothers, announcing the testament of God to you, I did not come with brilliance of speech or of wisdom. For I determined to know nothing among you except Jesus Christ and Him crucified (1 Cor. 2:1-2)."

The first thing one notes is **Paul's message**. Paul began the chapter with the phrase "When I," or in some translations, "and I." It also can be translated "accordingly." This phrase connects the thought to the previous verse. Remember that 1 Corinthians 1 ended with the idea that the only thing one may brag about is who one is in Jesus Christ. Jesus is the only important thing. So Paul said, "I could have come with flowery speech. I could have impressed you with brilliance. I could have attempted to win you over, but the reality is that the most important thing is not how well I say it, but what is being said."

There once was a church that had a beautiful stained glass window of Jesus directly behind the pulpit. The church's pastor was extremely tall, so he kept anyone from seeing the window because of his stature.

One Sunday, the lanky pastor was away on vacation. His replacement was a little smaller in stature, maybe a little vertically challenged. (I'm always interested in using the politically correct language "vertically challenged." I had someone who was short tell me that they were "vertically challenged." I said, "Yeah, and I'm not fat, I am horizontally enriched.") One of the little girls in the congregation asked, "Where is that man that keeps us from seeing Jesus every Sunday?"

God forbid that whoever stands in the pulpit prevents us from seeing Jesus Christ. Galatians 6:14 states, "But as for me, I will never boast about anything except the cross of our Lord Jesus Christ."

Richard Foster, in his book *Streams of Living Water*, tells about Billy Graham in his early years of ministry. In 1955 Graham was invited to Cambridge University and was asked to speak for an entire week. The first three nights, Graham determined that he would try to debate eloquently the truth of scripture, trying to impress the students at Cambridge. No one was impressed. So on the fourth night, Graham decided he would share the simplicity of the message of Jesus Christ. Richard Foster wrote, "The results were astonishing. Hundreds of sophisticated students responded to the clear presentation of the gospel having understood it for the very first time." It was a lesson in clarity and simplicity that Billy Graham never forgot. If you have ever heard Billy Graham's messages, you know that from 1955 forward, the simplicity of the gospel was his theme. A great old hymn challenges us, "Let others see Jesus in you. Keep telling the story. Be faithful and true. Let others see Jesus in you."[2]

Notice also **Paul's manner**. In 1 Corinthians 2:3-4, Paul reported he began sharing his message with "fear and trembling." His fear was not because of danger, but out of the awesome responsibility that he for communicating the gospel. I can still remember the very first sermon I preached. On a Youth Sunday in 1976, I, as a high school senior, was called upon to preach in my home church. I was frightened beyond measure. Many today have a hard time believing that I was a shy and reclusive teenager. I remember going over my message notes in a private room prior to the service. Our church's chairman of the deacons, Bill Flint, came in and said, "Mark, we are praying for you." Then he asked me, "Are you scared? Are you frightened?" I said, "I'm just about half out of my wits. I just don't know what to do." Mr.

Flint reassured me, saying, "Just remember this: fear indicates that you really care about what you are going to say." This piece of wisdom has always stuck with me; my prayer continues to be that I'll never let that holy sense of fear leave me. I hope always to be concerned about what I'm going to say. I always want to be overcome with the very awesome responsibility of teaching and preaching the truth.

The key to preaching is found in 1 Corinthians 2:4: "My speech and my proclamation were not with persuasive words of wisdom, but with a demonstration of the Spirit and of power." The key to preaching is not the power of persuasion. Any thing that I can talk you into, someone can talk you out of. Preaching is not the power of persuasion. Preaching should be the "demonstration of the Spirit."

Early in my ministry, during my very first pastorate in Mosheim, Tennessee, I contracted an eye infection. I couldn't see well enough to read my Bible. I made a valiant attempt to lead worship on Sunday morning, but we also had a Sunday night service and I knew there was no way that I would be able to survive a second service. I called the one pastor in the county whom I knew well enough to ask, "Is there anyone that you are aware of who would be available to preach for me on short notice?" He said, "I have two or three 'preacher boys' in my church who have surrendered to the ministry and are just beginning to receive training. I will send one of them over to you this evening."

Now I'm not poking fun, I'm just explaining the appearance of my last-minute pulpit supply. He had plaid pants, a striped shirt, a polka-dot tie, and a checkerboard jacket. I looked at him and thought, "Oh, God, please let me still be pastor of this church come tomorrow." The young pulpiteer brought with him an entire year's worth of notes from his pastor's lessons on the Holy Spirit on Wednesday nights. He stood up with that entire year's worth of notes. He preached through a page, lick his finger, and flip a page. I know more about the Holy Spirit having heard that one sermon than probably any other sermon I've ever heard. He preached for over an hour. Finally, after having gone through pages and pages of notes, the young man said, "I'm not going to be able to reach the conclusion, but let me give an invitation right now." I sighed to myself, "Oh, thank God!"

A lady who had arrived during the sermon was sitting in the back pew. He asked for people who would be willing to respond to Jesus

Christ. She came down the aisle, tears running down her face, and gave her life to Jesus Christ. It wasn't about the way the preacher was dressed. It wasn't about the eloquence of the preacher's speech. But it *was* about the simplicity of the message of Jesus Christ that had grabbed her heart. God demonstrated what his Spirit can do.

The third thing to consider about Paul's approach to the gospel was **his motive**. In 1 Corinthians 2:5, he wrote, "...so that your faith might not be based on men's wisdom but on God's power." Paul wanted them to put their trust in the demonstration of God's Spirit and not in the explanation of a man. All of us know smooth-talking people who could sell water to a drowning person. But in reality, proclamation is not about the eloquence of speech. I once heard a story of a man with alcoholism who gave his life to Christ. His drinking buddies said, "Do you really believe all that stuff in the Bible? Do you really believe that Jesus turned water into wine?" The reformed man responded, "I don't know about that, but if you'll come over to my house I'll show you how he turned beer into furniture." The demonstration of a changed life was what Paul was all about.

This **message** of Christ that we are purchased by the Son is extended in the simplicity of the cross, the sacrifice made in a **manner** to draw attention to Jesus with a **motive** to ground believers in truth and to change their lives.

This Message was Planned by the Father

The gospel is simple—so simple that a child can understand it. But it is also so complex that the theologians of the ages have never been able to comprehend it all. The gospel is about a God who loves us intimately. The message is that the Son has purchased our salvation, working out the plan the Father had made before the beginning.

This is something only **comprehended by the mature.** 1 Corinthians 2:6 states, "However, among the mature we do speak a wisdom, but not a wisdom of this age, or of the rulers of this age, who are coming to nothing." I know some translations use the word "perfect." This translation actually refers to a word that literally means "mature." It describes people who are "getting it," people who are "into it."

In the early church there were two kinds of instruction. First there was *kerygma*. This means "an announcement." It means to tell the facts. We would call it the news—the "who, what, when, where, why and how." Some people know all the facts about the church, all the facts about Christianity. The second word for instruction is *didache*, meaning "teaching." It entails interpreting. It's the explanation of the meaning of the facts. Paul said there were people who needed to move beyond the facts of Christianity to knowing the heart behind the facts.

This plan, comprehended only by the mature, is **concealed in mystery**: "On the contrary, we speak God's hidden wisdom in a mystery, which God predestined before the ages for our glory. None of the rulers of this age knew it, for if they had known it, they would not have crucified the Lord of Glory" (1 Cor. 2:7-8).

How good are you at keeping a secret? Secrets are fun to hear. They are no fun to keep. God has told us a mystery, a secret. The New Testament period mystery religions proliferated. Some people thought Christianity was just another one of the mystery religions. Mystery religions were based upon learning the secrets; knowing those secrets moved you up the ladder to heaven. After all, Jesus taught in parables: "Then the disciples came up and asked Him, 'Why do you speak to us in parables?' He answered them, 'Because the secrets of the kingdom of Heaven have been given for you to know, but it has not been given to them'" (Matt. 13:10-11). People surmised, "I just need to get into the inner circle of understanding the secrets." According to 1 Corinthians 2:8, the "rulers of this age" did not get the secrets. There are two interpretations of the identity of these rulers. Some believe they were the political leaders of the day; certainly the world leaders in the first century did not get the message of Jesus. Others interpret the "rulers of this age" as demonic powers. The Bible also teaches that the demonic powers did not understand the message of Jesus.

Christianity, however, is not a mystery religion like other mystery religions, because the secrets were all clearly given to Christians, who have been told to share them with others. Jesus basically says, "Let me tell you a secret and let me give you the privilege of telling others the secret. Let me commission you that you tell everybody you come in contact with the secret that I have given to you."

This message comprehended only by the mature and concealed in mystery is **colossal to man.** 1 Corinthians 2:9 actually cites Isaiah 64:4, "What no eye has seen, no ear has heard, what has never come into man's heart is what God has prepared for those who love him." God's plan is infinite. Eyes cannot see it all, ears cannot hear it all, and the mind cannot comprehend it all. It's like the potato chip commercial that says, "Nobody can eat just one." If you ever taste God's grace, if you ever taste God's goodness, you'll never be satisfied with anything less. Some people think they've seen it all. Some people think they've heard it all. Some people think they've experienced it all. They think they have God in a box. God is so far beyond that.

The Message was Publicized by the Spirit

Did you realize that salvation involves all three parts of the Godhead—God the Father, God the Son, and God the Holy Spirit? 1 Peter 1:2 states that Christians are the elect, "...according to the foreknowledge of God the Father through sanctification of the Spirit unto obedience of the sprinkling of the blood of Jesus Christ." Our salvation began when God elected us by grace before the foundation of the world. Jesus died for us so that we could come to him. And the Holy Spirit convicts us and regenerates us by drawing us to the Father.

In the conclusion of 1 Corinthians 2, Paul cited four works of God's Spirit. The first one is that the **Spirit discloses**. Verse 10 says that the Spirit discloses, "...the deep things of God." Perhaps someone has come to you and said, "Can I pick your brain?" Maybe he or she wanted to say, "Can I have your innermost thoughts? Can I have what you are really thinking about this?" Some may know the facts about you. They may know your name, your family, your address, and where you like to go on vacation. But do they really know you? James 2:19 states, "You believe that God is one; you do well. The demons also believe and they shudder." Even the Devil and all his demons know the facts about Jesus. But 1 Corinthians 2:11 says, "For who among men knows the concerns of a man except the Spirit of a man that is in him? In the same way, no one knows the concerns of God except the Spirit of God." The only person who can reveal the innermost thoughts of you is you. And the only person that can reveal the innermost heart of God is God. The very first work of the Holy Spirit is that he discloses to us the very heart of God.

The Holy Spirit not only discloses, the Spirit also **dwells.** In 1 Corinthians 2:12, Paul wrote, "Now we have not received the spirit of the world, but the Spirit who is from God, in order to know what has been freely given to us by God." The Holy Spirit lives within us, as the epistle notes: "Do you not know that your body is a sanctuary of the Holy Spirit who is in you, whom you have from God? You are not your own, for you were bought at a price; therefore glorify God in your body" (1 Cor. 6:19-20). At the time of your conversion, when you gave your life to Christ, God's Spirit possessed you. God's Spirit now dwells within you. He has taken up permanent residence.

The Holy Spirit discloses and dwells; it also directs: "We also speak these things, not in words taught by human wisdom, but in those taught by the Spirit, explaining spiritual things to spiritual people" (1 Cor. 2:13). Jesus promised his disciples before his imminent death that there would be another who would come—a comforter. According to John's gospel, Jesus said, "And he will teach you all things and bring all things to your remembrance" (John 14:26). In other words, God provided for us our own GPS system, our personal directive system. As the gospel writer notes, "When he, the Spirit of truth, is come, he will guide you into all truth: for he shall not speak of himself; but whatsoever he shall hear, that shall he speak: and he will show you things to come. He shall glorify me" (John 16:13, KJV) The Spirit never draws attention to himself; He always diverts attention to Christ. The Spirit always directs us into the way of Jesus.

The final work of the Spirit 1 Corinthians 2 discloses is that the Spirit **develops.** Paul introduced two types of people in the final paragraph. The first is the natural man or *psuchikos*. This term gives us the word "physical." It means "those who only follow after physical desires." The second word is *pneumatikai*, meaning spiritual. The "spirit man" does not follow after the natural ways. 1 Corinthians 2:15 states that the spirit man is able to evaluate or judge. The Spirit is able to estimate or to scrutinize. In the next verse, Paul writes, "For who has known the Lord's mind, that he may instruct Him? But we have the mind of Christ." The only way to evaluate effectively is to have the mind of Christ. This facility develops over time. In years with my precious wife, Glenda, I've learned a great deal. I think I could now order for her in a restaurant. I think I know her favorite colors. This is knowledge I have developed because of our relationship, because of time spent together. Paul was telling the Corinthians: the only way to deal with your difficulties is to develop a relationship with Jesus Christ.

I have just completed the forty-day study, *The Love Dare*. The book is a product inspired by the movie *Fire Proof*. I have been studying about how to be a better husband and trying to do "The Love Dare." When I came to the fortieth day I found it to be a most insightful and most challenging time.

The Bible compares the relationship of a husband and a wife with the relationship of Christ with the church. According to Ephesians 5:25: "Husbands, love your wives, just as also Christ loved the church and gave Himself for her." The challenge for men is that they ought to love their wives in the same fashion and the same manner that Christ loved the church. How did Christ love the church? He loved the church in a covenant relationship. The word *covenant* appears repeatedly throughout the Bible in telling how God relates to his people. In Genesis 9, God entered into a covenant with Noah, promising never again to destroy the earth. In Genesis 17, God entered into a covenant with Abraham, assuring that his descendents would become a great nation. In Exodus 19, God entered into a covenant with Moses, promising that the people of Israel would always be God's personal and permanent possession. In 2 Samuel 7, God entered into a covenant with David, and said that there would always be a ruler who would set upon God's throne forever.

Then in the New Testament in Hebrews 9, God entered into a new covenant with the church that all who believe in the sacrifice the Son of God, Jesus, would spend eternity with him in Heaven. We have problems with relationships today because we have replaced covenants with contracts.

There is a huge difference between a contract and a covenant. For example, a contract is written because of distrust. It outlines consequences of not living up to the agreement. By contrast a covenant is based upon trust. Its purpose is unconditional and is expressed in extreme love. A contract asks, "How does this affect me?" The key is to limit my liability. It is an opportunity to protect myself. But a covenant says, "How can I touch the lives of others?" Its key is to extend responsibility beyond limitations with no expirations. A contract is broken by mutual consent. That is why one in two marriages in America ends in divorce. Most people view marriage as contractual. But a covenant is unbreakable. It is a permanent relationship.

Ephesians 5:25 proclaims, "Husbands love your wives just as also Christ loved the church." Marriage is to be a covenant relationship because Christianity is a covenant relationship. God loves us in a covenant relationship; we are then to love God in a covenant relationship.

Paul said that if you want the church to come together, if you want the church to be unified in its purpose, and if you want to work well together, then don't follow human advice about organizations. Instead, seek to get on the same page with others and join together in a covenant relationship with God.

LESSON 3
GROWING THE
CHURCH GOD'S
WAY

There was a huge movement that swept across the United States in the 1970s and '80s, known as the "church growth movement." This movement promoted the principles to become a multiplying church. In that time, one image shared repeatedly in the classroom was that the church was a living organism and should naturally grow. Any living organism that stops growing begins to die. People asked, "What should a growing church look like?" Three basic attributes a growing church emerged. One was that growing churches were building buildings. Facilities became extremely important to the church. Statistics proved that when a building use reached 80 percent of capacity then no one else would come. Therefore, churches began to build bigger buildings. Facilities now account for 20 percent of church expenditures in almost every church in the United States. In addition, 54 percent of churches in the United States currently carry a debt because of these buildings.[1] The church believed the adage "If you build it, they will come."

The second attribute of church growth was budgets. Reggie McNeal is the director of church health for the Southern Baptist Convention in South Carolina. In his book, *The Present Future*, McNeal states that Christian churches in America spend $1.5 million for every person they lead to the Lord Jesus Christ.[2] Did you get that? So churches have ballooned their buildings and their budgets.

A third way we began to count church growth was just in bodies. It was a matter of filling up the sanctuary, packing the pews. After

9/11, church attendance across the United States hit an all-time high; 47 percent of people said that they were attending church regularly immediately after 9/11. That is the highest percentage in the past 100 years. There has been, however, a slow decline ever since then.[3]

Since the 1970s a generation has been measuring church growth by buildings, budgets, and body counts. Has the church been making inroads into the social decline of our society? The American church is struggling, to the point of being anemic. Less than 1 percent of churches are expanding by what is called "conversion growth." C. Peter Wagner, longtime professor of church growth at Fuller Theological Seminary, said, "There is no county across the nation that has had a net growth in Christianity in the last two decades."[4] There is no county in America that is more Christian today than it was twenty years ago! Now more than ever we need to "be the church." Rick Warren, author of *The Purpose Driven Life*, said, "I agree that the key issue for churches in the twenty-first century will not be church growth it will be church health."[5] When a congregation is healthy, it will grow. God desires for his church to grow. Therefore, the key is for churches to become healthy and reap the natural benefits of church health through dynamic church growth. That leads us to ask what Paul said about growing the early New Testament church in Corinth.

Paul didn't say anything about church buildings, he didn't say anything about church budgets; and he didn't say anything about counting the number of people that attends worship services. But he did give three illustrations. He gave an illustration of an **analyst** who teaches us about how to grow in maturity. He used the illustration of an **agriculturalist** teaching how to grow in quantity. The final illustration Paul used pointed to an **architect** who teaches how to grow in quality.

The Illustration of an Analyst

The first illustration is of an **analyst**. In 1 Corinthians 2, Paul divided people into two categories, natural and spiritual. *Natural* described people who were pursuing physical desires. Among the others pursuing spiritual desires, Paul saw two groups: mature and immature. Some believers were immature because they simply hadn't been saved very long before. They were just getting into Bible study and learning God's plans for their lives.

A new Christian in my church told me she had started reading the book of Job, because she needed a job. I explained to her that the name of the book is Jōb, named after the book's primary character. She said, "Well, I noticed it was right after this wonderful book of poetry called palms." I informed her that it is really called Psalms. You may not know Job from job or Psalms from palms because of how long you have been a believer.

Others are immature because their growth has been stunted. Paul said there were two identifying marks of maturity in a believer. First is a **proper diet**. You may have heard people say, "You are what you eat." You need to have a balanced diet. After the first of the year everyone makes that New Year's resolution to begin eating right and exercising. A proper diet according to the food pyramid has a variety of food groups in proportionate amounts. Think about how this applies to babies. A baby should grow naturally and should progress from a diet of milk to one of solid foods. But if a baby remains on milk for too long, that baby can become bloated, lifeless, and unhealthy. There is nothing wrong with milk. It is just not the proper diet for an extended period of time. This raises the question, "Can there ever be too much of a good thing?" People could live on good things, but for too long a time. For example, individuals may understand Bible stories and basic things that are good for them, but never advance to what is described in 1 Corinthians 2 as the "deep things of God." It gladdens the heart of every pastor when people want to be enlightened and they want to be taught. It is interesting that immature Christians described in 1 Corinthians 3 are not people feeding on garbage, things harmful to their spiritual walks. Instead they are feeding upon good things, but not the "best things" for them. One of the marks of maturity is seeking after the deep things of God and getting a properly balanced spiritual diet.

A second mark of maturity is a **positive disposition.** 1 Corinthians 3:3 says, "Because you are still fleshly for since there is envy and strife among you, you that are not fleshly, live like ordinary people but for whoever someone says, 'I'm with Paul' and another, 'I'm with Apollos,' are you not typically men?" The mature person is one who seeks to get along with other people. Immature people love to fuss with one another. You don't have to be around children for very long to realize that fussing comes naturally for them. We are born with a selfish nature, a "my way" mentality. We have learned that there were factions within this Corinthian church, with divisions over who was to be the leader. What appears here is a passage that seems to read something like, "My dad can beat up your dad." That is the way that immaturity plays itself out. Paul responded to this debate over immaturity, writing, "What is Paul and what is Apollos but servants?" Some translations say "Who is Paul and who is Apollos." That choice of translation seems to communicate, "Who do they think they are, or who do you think they are?"

A more accurate translation would say, "What are they?" This identifies the reason that God has placed these spiritual leaders in our lives. They are placed to be examples of servanthood. "What are Paul and Apollos, but servants?" The word servant is the word *diakonoi,* from which we get our word "deacon." I am very proud of the deacons at my church, Northside Baptist Church. They genuinely want to be examples of a servant spirit. They do not serve in "limelight" ministries. Instead, they serve in everyday capacities so that they might be examples of servanthood to the entire fellowship. The Bible declares that the greatest leaders are ones who serve. One of the ways to have a positive disposition is by serving others. You may have heard the old cliché, "Those who are rowing the boat usually don't have time to complain about where they are going."

So the first example is that of an Analyst who teaches us about the growth and maturity that we need to seek a proper diet. We need to get beyond the simplicity of the message of the gospel to dig for the deep things of God. We need to have a positive disposition that can only come with having a servant heart and a servant spirit.

The Illustration of an Agriculturalist

The second example is an **agriculturalist**. Paul was fond of agricultural metaphors; in 1 Corinthians 3:9, he wrote, "You are God's field." In another translation, his words appear as "You are God's husbandry." The word appearing as *field* or *husbandry* means *garden.* I've never known anyone who grew a garden who wasn't proud of it, whether it was a flower garden or a vegetable garden. Gardeners want to take people to their gardens and show them off. I believe that God takes great pride in the church being his garden. We are God's field. Through this metaphor of an agriculturalist, Paul teaches us three principles.

First of all there is **diversity in our assignments**. 1Corinthians 3:6 states, "I planted, Apollos watered but God gave the growth." Later in chapters 12, 13, and 14, Paul mentioned that there was a diversity of spiritual gifts found in the body of Christ. Not everyone has the same gifts, but God has given each person gifts so that we might minister within the body to one another. Romans 12:4-5 says, "Now, as we have many parts in one body, and all the parts do not have the same function, in the same way we who are many are one body in Christ and individually members of one another." The Bible teaches that we have this diversity among us so that we might be able to minister to one another. Therefore, we each need to recognize our parts and then play them. It is like playing in a marching band. Different instruments have different sounds and they have different parts to play. Musicians need to recognize their assigned parts and play them. Warren Wiersbe once said, "Spiritual gifts are tools to build with and not toys to play."[6] There is obviously diversity in assignments.

The second principle points out that church members need **unity in our aim**. Paul, Apollos, and Peter were not competing with one another. They were completing one another. They were completing the work of the church. I have had the wonderful privilege of serving as a senior pastor for twenty-eight years. I have calculated that I have witnessed about a thousand baptisms in my churches during that period of time. I know that in many of those situations someone else planted before me and I just had the wonderful opportunity of coming behind them watering and was present at harvest time. I pray that I am also currently planting seeds; that others will water and reap the harvest. This is not competition but a completion. That is why we need always to be scattering the seed.

There's diversity in our assignments and unity in our aim. Thirdly, there is **humility in our action**. 1 Corinthians 3:7 says, "So that neither the one that plants nor the one who waters is anything but only God who gives the growth." Does a farmer really have any say over how fast crops grow? The farmer can be faithful in the field, but the growth is still up to God. It is God's timing and it is God's harvest. 2 Corinthians 6:1-2 says, "Working together with Him, we also appeal to you. Don't receive God's grace in vain for He says in an acceptable time I heard you; and in the day of salvation, I helped you. Look, now is the acceptable time look now is the day of salvation." God knows when it is harvest time. Acts 2:47 says, "And every day the Lord added to them those who were being saved." If God knows when it is harvest time, what is our personal responsibility? Our personal responsibility is to be faithful in the field. There can be no excuse for laziness. According to Proverbs 24:30-34, "I went by the field of a slacker, by the vineyard of a man who was lacking sense. Thistles came up everywhere, weeds covered the ground and the stone wall was ruined. I saw and took it to heart; I looked and received instruction: a little sleep, a little slumber, a little floating of arms to rest, and your poverty will come like a robber, your need like a bandit." An analyst teaches us about growth and maturity. An agriculturalist teaches about growth and quantity. God is the harvester, but we have to be faithful in the field.

The Illustration of the Architect

There's a third illustration here. It is the illustration of an **architect** and it teaches us about growth in quality. Paul also referred to the church metaphorically as God's building. The phrase implies edifying or building up and is translated in other portions of the New Testament by those words. How does one build up the church of God? If God is the harvester and all happens in God's time and all is under God's control, what is God asking of us? What is "building up" the church of God? In Ephesians 2:18-22, Paul discussed this formula of building up the church of God. He wrote,

> For through Him we both have access by one spirit
> to the Father. So then you are no longer foreigners
> and strangers, but fellow citizens with the saints, and
> members of God's household, built on the foundation
> of the apostles and prophets with Christ Jesus Himself

as the cornerstone. The whole building is being fitted together in Him and is growing into a holy sanctuary in the Lord, in whom you are also being built together for God's dwelling in the Spirit.

There are three important phrases in that passage. The first refers to the **foundation**. The prophets' and apostles' teaching concerning Jesus formed the foundation of the church. The "fitting together" meant the framework of how the church bound Christians together in worship and spirit.

I have seen people try to build churches on improper foundations, including, for example, pulpit personalities, musical programming, and even specific doctrines. These are all fatally faulty foundations. As an illustration of this mistake, consider the story of Bennano Pisano, the Italian architect, commissioned in 1173 to do the greatest work of his life—an eight-story bell tower for the cathedral in the city of Pisa. This would have been the pinnacle of his career, but unfortunately, the great architect had forgotten the most important element—the foundation. Not going down deep enough to lay a secure foundation, the Tower of Pisa was built. It took 176 years to be completed. It took so long to finish because soon after beginning the project, workers began to notice that the tower was starting to lean. As each story was added, builders attempted to straighten the tower and strengthen the foundation. The finished product became a visible example of a failed foundation. It leans to an increasing degree every year; now it is almost thirteen feet off of center with a pitch of almost four degrees. Though it has stood for over 800 years, every architect in the world says it is condemned to fall...eventually. After being closed to tourists because of the danger of collapse, the tower was straightened and strengthened and is now open to tourists.

A proper foundation must be laid before any building can take place. In Matthew 16:15, Jesus asked his disciples,

> "But you, who do you say that I am?" Simon Peter, (speaking on behalf of the Twelve) answered, "You are the Messiah, the Son of the living God," and Jesus responded, "Simon, son of Jonah, you are blessed because flesh and blood did not reveal this to you but

> my Father in heaven; and I also say to you that you are Peter and on this rock (meaning the rock of Jesus Christ) I will build my church."

Peter, you understand, you get it, and you have laid the right foundation. You can build your life correctly if you understand that the foundation is Jesus Christ.

Jesus also told a parable that illustrates the same message:

> Therefore, if everyone hears these words of Mine and acts on them will be like a sensible man who built his house on the rock. The rain fell and the rivers rose and the winds blew and pounded that house. Yet it didn't collapse, because its foundation was upon the rock. But everyone who hears these words of Mine and doesn't act on them is like a foolish man who built his house on the sand. The rain fell, the rivers rose, the winds blew and pounded that house and it collapsed. And its collapse was great (Matt. 7:24-29).

We sing, "On Christ the solid rock I stand, all other ground is sinking sand." Paul said, "I am a master builder," in 1 Corinthians 3:10. The phrase "master builder" bears the meaning of a superintendent, an overseer. This means that Paul actually was not in the building project or in the city of Corinth. Paul had ministered in the city for a year and a half. The only place he'd spent more time was in the city of Ephesus, where he ministered for three years. Most places Paul only had the opportunity to stay a month or two at best, just enough time to lay a proper foundation of teaching.

After a proper foundation, Paul advanced to the **framework** of the church. He explained how the church was formed and fitted together. 1 Corinthians 3:12 says, "If anyone builds upon the foundation with gold and silver and costly stones, wood, hay or straw, each one's work will become obvious for the day will declare." How was the church fitted together? If one wanted to .do quality work, one needed to use quality products. Many times this passage is interpreted to refer to the works of the church. "Wood, hay, and straw," which will be consumed by the flames of judgment, are compared to "gold, silver, and costly stones," which withstand the fire. The church recog its work as eternal.

Could this passage also be referring to the doctrines of the church? Where does one find "wood, hay, and straw?" Anywhere. Many people try to fill the church with anything that they can get from anywhere they can find it. Instead, "gold, silver, and costly stones" ought to be brought into the church. Where does one find those things? One must dig for them. The framework of the church is a group of people digging for the deep things of God, the precious things of God, the "gold, silver, and costly stones" that only God can place into their lives. This comes by understanding what God intends for them rather than anything that the world has to offer them. Quality work demands quality products.

Paul said that the foundation of the church was the message of Christ and the framework was the engaged membership. Then Paul pointed out the **filling** of the church. 1 Corinthians 3:16 says, "Don't you know that you are God's sanctuary?" Emphatically, "Don't you know that you are actually the church? Don't you realize that?" *You* are the church. The church does not exist at an address. The church does not exist in buildings and bricks and mortar. *You* are the sanctuary. 1 Corinthians 3:17 declares, "If anyone ruins God's sanctuary, God will ruin him." If anyone tries to destroy the church (the fellowship), God will destroy him or her. A Spirit-filled church recognizes that Satan is at work. Someone once told me the devil isn't fighting the church anymore; he has just joined it. Most churches are very much aware of the spiritual warfare taking place in their lives.

Paul called the Corinthians to be wise, to realize that they were God's church. They were the sanctuary. Paul wrote, "No one should deceive himself. If anyone among you thinks he is wise in this age he must become foolish so that he may become wise" (1 Cor. 3:18). An ancient proverb says, "He who knows not and knows not that he knows not is a fool; stay away from him. But he that knows not and knows that he knows not is a wise man, stand beside him and teach him." The only individuals who know the wisdom of God are those open to being taught by the Spirit of God. Unfortunately, numerous churches have not allowed this to take place.

...rd, a University of Southern California sociologist, ...he demise of the church in America. "By the middle ...ieth) century, (the church) had lost any recognized, ...logically, and psychologically sound approach to ...to becoming like Christ."[7] The church has become so enamored with numerical growth that we have forgotten that the purpose of growing the church is for people to become like Christ. Growing the church God's way is a decision: "I want to become like Christ. I want to become so contagious in spirit that someone else might want to become like Christ. The more I become like Christ the more I will 'be the church.' Being the church will grow the church." The ministry of the church is to grow up in maturity, to grow out in quantity, and to grow strong in quality.

Paul concluded this chapter by saying, "So no one should boast in men, for all things are yours: whether Paul or Apollos or Cephas or the world or life or death or things present or things to come—all are yours, and you belong to Christ and Christ to God" (1 Cor. 3:21-23). Paul reiterated that the only thing we have to brag about is Christ.

One of my favorite hymns from my boyhood included these lines: "Now I belong to Jesus. Jesus belongs to me. Not for the years of time alone but for eternity." Growing the church God's way may or may not include constructing buildings, breaking record budgets, or gathering an enormous number of bodies to praising the Redeemer. When the church grows God's way, however, it continually will develop a deepening dependence upon belonging to Him. "I am His and He is mine forever and forever!"

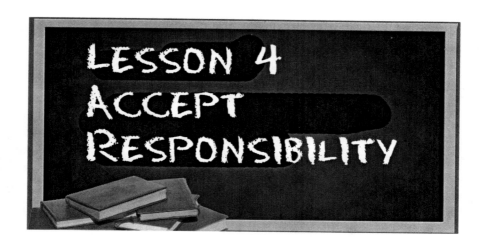

LESSON 4
ACCEPT
RESPONSIBILITY

I f you know that you belong to the Lord Jesus Christ and Christ belongs to you, then you are very much prepared for the fourth lesson, which is to **accept your responsibility**. John Fitzgerald Kennedy, in his 1961 inauguration speech, said, "Ask not what your country can do for you," but what? "Ask what you can do for your country." I watched the inauguration of President Barak Obama with our church's senior adult luncheon group. We had the big screen television in our church's fellowship area tuned to the historic event and I thought, "What will be the memorable phrase that will surface out of this inauguration? What will be the memorable phrase that will be quoted a decade from now?" History remembers President Kennedy's great inauguration speech. An older generation recalls Franklin Delano Roosevelt saying, "We have nothing to fear but fear itself." So what will be the catch phrase? I tried to analyze the speech as I listened.

President Obama called for a "new era of responsibility." The front page of the Indianapolis Star the next day had this quote from the speech: "Starting today, we must pick ourselves up, dust ourselves off, and begin again, the work of remaking America."[1] He issued a call for us to accept our responsibility. Now, that's not new among politicians. It is something that has been tested—tried and true—for generations. Folksy President Harry S. Truman had a desk plate on his oval office desk that read, "The Buck Stops Here." Truman didn't invent that phrase, although many people thought that he had. It is actually an old poker term. The dollar "chip" is passed around the table to determine who has the deal. Who is going to deal the cards the next time around? Someone asks, "Who's responsible for this?" It is the person before whom the dollar chip, the buck, is resting; the buck stops here. Harry Truman was saying people are passing the buck. People are continually trying to blame someone else for what's gone wrong in their lives. Truman was claiming, "I'm willing to take responsibility because the buck stops here."

I shared this because I knew many of you would not know a poker analogy, being good church-going people. Come to think of it, Harry Truman was a good Southern Baptist who enjoyed a spirited game of poker. This was his way of stating, "I accept my responsibility."

Peter Drucker, the leadership guru, defines a leader this way: "a leader is one who has followers. An effective leader is not someone who is loved or admired necessarily; he is someone whose followers do the right thing."[2] Popularity is not at the core of leadership; results are. Leaders are highly visible; they therefore set examples. And leadership is not about rank or privilege, titles or money; leadership means responsibility. A leader is someone who has followers; leadership is accepting responsibility.

Have you ever noticed that if you give people responsibility they tend to care more about results? You may have noticed that in a Sunday School class. If you give someone the responsibility of bringing the snack or making the coffee or leading the prayer time, suddenly they care much more because they own the responsibility. It's a tried and true principle that people care about items for which they are responsible.

This means not just saying you are responsible; it means accepting the responsibility. For instance, 96 percent of parents of children under the age of thirteen say that they are responsible for teaching their children values. These parents say we own that responsibility; we accept that responsibility. However, less than 50 percent of them have had any conversation discussing religious matters with their children in any given week.[3] Often times we say we accept responsibility, but we don't do it. If we belong to Christ, then we must accept the responsibility that goes with belonging to Him.

The Role of a Steward of God

You might ask, "Now that I have given my life to Christ, what does God want with me?" There are three responsible roles I want to share with you. The first role is that of being a **steward of God.** In 1 Corinthians 4:1, Paul described the followers as "servants." Some translations use the word "ministers." This literally is a word that meant to be an "under-rower." It was the picture word of slaves who would row the ships; the great Roman galleys. Paul said that the Corinthians were not the captains of the ship, but rather the slaves, the under-rowers. The church does, however, have some management. Christians are the managers of God's household. The King James Version uses the word "steward." This means that Christians are not owners of anything, but are steward, placed in charge of things. Galatians 6:10 states, "As we have opportunity, we must work for the good of all, especially those who belong to the household of faith." One might think that perhaps the most important qualification for someone to be a steward, the manager of a household, would be that he or she would be a hard worker or administratively minded. But the most important quality of a steward is to be found faithful.

Most Americans were made aware that a "slip up" happened during the inauguration of President Obama as he was reciting of the oath of office. The mix up happened with the words "faithfully execute." Chief Justice Roberts misplaced that phrase the first time he said it. Consequently, they repeated the swearing in a second time that evening, just to be sure that it was said precisely and to offer an "abundance of precaution" against legal loopholes. There was a genuine fear of potential trouble if President Obama did not say the exact words present in the Constitution of the United States. Jay Leno, in his opening monologue that evening on the Tonight Show, said, "Is it any surprise to us? Politicians for years have choked on the word 'faithfully.'" It is not just politicians who choke on the word 'faithfully.' It is required of stewards that all are found faithful.

Jesus tells the story in Luke 16 of a "shrewd steward." In the end, however, the steward was dismissed because he was dishonest. He had not been faithful. If we are stewards, managers of God's household, to whom are we accountable? Romans 14:4 explains, "Who are you to criticize another's household slave? Before his own Lord he stands or falls." A steward is accountable to his or her own master. We are accountable to God.

So how are we to evaluate faithfulness? Paul described three different types of evaluations. First is **peer evaluation**. Paul wrote, "It is of little importance that I should be evaluated by you or by human court" (1 Cor. 4:3). The phrase "human court" is literally a Greek word that means "man's day" (as opposed to the Lord's Day in judgment). Each person deserves a day in court, but often we allow what others think rather than what God thinks about us to rule our lives. Human court actually happens every day of our lives. It's not just when we've done something wrong. We are always aiming to please others. We are always aiming to be in style, in fashion, in vogue. Paul explained that it was of little importance what a human court says about an individual. It is not very important. He did not say that it was of no importance; he said it was of little importance. Certainly protecting one's reputation has some importance. There is some importance in what others think about an individual, but those thoughts are not the most important thing. To paraphrase, Paul said, "If you are debating about who is the best preacher in the world, I really don't care whether you put me at the top of your list."

The second type of evaluation is **personal evaluation**. 1 Corinthians 4:3-4 says, in essence, "In fact. I don't even evaluate myself, for I am not conscious of anything against myself, but I'm not justified by this." When I begin to evaluate myself, two extremes may cause me difficulty. Either I am too hard on myself or I am too easy on myself. Some people are just too hard on themselves. They are unable to forgive themselves. They are unable to get past their past. These people live persistently in the past tense. 1 John 3:20 states, "If our heart condemn us, God is greater than our hearts and (He) knows all things." So those of you who are too hard on yourselves and never can forgive yourselves, just remember that God has forgiven you. That is your proper personal evaluation.

Others are too easy on themselves, unable to sense conviction; they live persistently in sin. These individuals rationalize their relationships with God by saying, "Well, I'm just as good as so and so; or I'm not as bad as so and so." One of my first jobs as a teenager was in a fast food establishment. The manager of that restaurant knew that I was preparing to go on to college and train for ministry. Often he would engage me in conversation, trying to challenge me on my system of beliefs. His infamous self-evaluation was, "I'm religious, I'm just not fanatical." I would ask, "What does that mean?" Everything depends upon where one stands. It is like the guy who is driving down the road and claims the highways are filled with maniacs and morons. A maniac is anyone driving faster than me; and anyone driving slower than me is a moron. One's view of fanaticism relates directly to where one stands with the Lord Jesus Christ. The common definition of fanaticism is anybody who's more hot-hearted, more zealous, and doing more for the cause of Christ than I am.

Peer evaluation and personal evaluation are just not sufficient. So what is sufficient? **Perfect evaluation**. 1 Corinthians 4:4-5 basically states, "The one who evaluates me is the Lord. Therefore don't judge anything prematurely before the Lord comes, who will both bring to light what is hidden in darkness and reveal the intentions of the hearts. And then praise will come to each one from God." Perfect evaluation is God's evaluation. 2 Corinthians 5:10 says, "For we must all appear before the judgment seat of Christ, so that each may be repaid for what he has done in the body, whether good or bad." God's evaluation of us is perfect for two reasons. First of all, his evaluation is based upon correct information. God reveals even the hidden things. They are brought into the light. We don't know all the truth until we know the author of truth.

Perfect evaluation is also based upon correct intentions. God is able to reveal the intentions of our hearts, not only what we have done, but also why we did it. You may have done the right thing for the wrong reason and still not be right. If I belong to Christ, I must be willing to accept the responsibility that I am a steward, a manager of God's household. As a manager of God's household, I am willing to be evaluated not merely by my peers and by me, but also to come under the evaluation of God.

The Role as a Spectacle of Glory

The second responsibility is to become a **spectacle of glory**. The passage says that we are spectacles to the world. The word *spectacle* relates to the Greek word *theatron*. This is the root for our English word "theatre." It was a common word used among the Greeks to describe when massive crowds would enter the coliseums. They came to see the Greek games, but then immediately after the games concluded, they would toss the poor and the imprisoned into the arena with wild animals. People would stay and watch the "spectacle" of it all, the *theatron* of it all. They would pour into the coliseums to watch people fighting for their lives. The world today is looking at you and me; they want to know what will motivate us to fight for our lives. We have become "spectacles" of the glory of God.

How do we become winners in these battles? The first thing is to recognize that we have **scriptural superiority**. 1 Corinthians 4:6 says,

> Now brothers, I have applied these things to myself and Apollos for your benefit so that you may learn from us the same nothing beyond what is written. The purpose is that none of you will be inflated with pride in favor of one person over another for who makes you so superior; what do you have that you didn't receive?

What makes you so superior? What makes you think that you can stand in the midst of all this? The only thing that allows me to have a position of superiority is the truth. We have nothing to be prideful about; we may brag of nothing except the superiority of Christ who is in us.

To be a winner, we need also to reject any **spiritual satisfaction**. 1 Corinthians 4:8 says, "Already you're full; already you're rich. You've begun to reign as kings without us and I wish you did reign so that we also could reign with you." Here Paul delved into some of the "sacred sarcasm" for which he is famous. Paul viewed the Corinthians as already "full," meaning "satisfied with food." In essence he was saying they were already a bunch of fat cats. Jesus, in his Sermon on the Mount, said, "Blessed are those who do hunger and thirst after righteousness for they are the ones that will be filled" (Matt. 5:6). Jesus commended people who recognized their spiritual hunger. The Corinthians, however, acted like that had arrived where they wanted to be and had accomplished this on their own. They had become pleased, proud, and pompous in their own selves and in their own way of doing things.

A guest preacher at the Southern Baptist Convention once made one of the most indicting statements that I have ever heard. People laughed at the time. His barb, however, was filled with stinging truth. This renowned pulpiteer said, "I am so grateful to be preaching to Southern Baptists today because of who you think you are." God forbid if we think of ourselves as anything apart from our identity in Jesus Christ.

We need to reject spiritual satisfaction. We need to recognize our scriptural superiority. To be a spectacle of God's glory we need also to realize our **saintly situation**. The world gave two descriptions to the early apostles. First, people in the world described them as "fools." Some thought of them as fools because of what they believed. Some people will think you are a fool because of your faith. Titus 2:14 states, "Jesus gave himself for us that He might redeem us from all inequity and purify unto Himself a peculiar people, zealous of good works" (KJV). Isn't it interesting that, in several places in the Bible, believers are referred to as "peculiar people?" I have met some believers who definitely are more peculiar than others. The world looks at us and says, "You fools." Henry David Thoreau once wrote, " If a man loses pace with his companions, perhaps it is because he hears a different drummer."[4] If you are going to be accused of being a fool, let it be because you have become a follower of Jesus Christ. In Matthew 5:22, Jesus said, "Whoever says to his brother, 'Fool!' will be subject the Sanhedrin. But whoever says, 'You moron!' will be subject to hellfire." It was considered to be a tremendous insult. But if anyone is a fool, let him be a fool for following Jesus Christ.

A second description of the early followers was that they were the filth of the world. In 1 Corinthians 4:13, believers in Christ were referred to as the "world's garbage heap." A modern paraphrase might refer to them as the "scum of the earth." You have been treated in the same way that the Lord Jesus Christ was treated. You have been treated as an outcast; you've been treated as if you don't belong; you've been treated like this world doesn't know what to do with you. If you are going to accept your responsibility of belonging to Christ, you must be willing to become a spectacle of his glory. When the world mistreats me; I will continue to stand for what Christ would have me stand for.

The Role as Sons of the Gospel

The third responsibility of believers is to be **sons (and daughters) of the gospel**. The June 2003 issue of Family Circle magazine reported on a national survey of fathers across the United States. The article stated that 94 percent of fathers felt building a family was the hardest and yet the most important thing they did. Seventy-one percent said fatherhood is more demanding than they expected. And 88 percent said it was also more rewarding than expected. While 90 percent said that becoming a father made them want to be a better person and a better role model for their children, 75 percent said they felt the weight of responsibility that they had never felt before.[5] The conclusion is clear. Fatherhood comes with weighty responsibilities. Paul looked at the early Corinthian church with the eyes of a spiritual father wanting to give sage advice: "I have led many of you into your salvation relationship. I have seen many of you birthed into the kingdom; but now, like a good dad, I want to accept some responsibility to teach you." Then he went on to describe some ways that they needed to learn.

First, they needed to **learn by explanation**. 1 Corinthians 4:14 states, "I'm not writing this to shame you but to warn you as my dear children for you have 10,000 instructors in Christ." That word "to warn" is used to describe how a father would warn his children. It is the same word appearing as "admonitions," meaning "warning of the Lord," used in Ephesians 6:4, "Fathers bring up your children in the nurture and admonitions" (KJV). Paul was saying "As a father in the gospel to you, I want to warn you, to instruct you, because there are 10,000 instructors competing for your attention." The word "instructor" literally means "child leader." There were 10,000 child leaders pulling for the attention of every man, woman, boy and girl in the land. They were trying to turn the people's heads, to move the Corinthian Christians to the leaders' opinions. There are few people who truly will act as fathers in life. We need to look for spiritual mentors, people whom we can trust, to whom we can give our fullest attention. We need to learn by explanations passed on to us from trusted figures.

The second step for the Christians at Corinth was to **learn by example**. 1 Corinthians 4:16 states, "Therefore I urge you be imitators of me." Some translations use the word "follower." It is literally a word that means "to mimic," like playing "Follow the Leader." I want you to be an imitator; I want you to follow me. I used to see bumper stickers that said, "Follow me to…" and you could just fill in the blank. "Follow me to Myrtle Beach, SC." "Follow me to Gatlinburg, TN." I even saw churches that used these bumper stickers. "Follow me to Northside Baptist Church." My questions for you are these: "If someone were to follow you, where would he or she end up? If someone were to become an imitator of you, to mimic you, where would he or she end up?" Don't just be a good follower, but also realize that there may be people following you. Be a good leader.

Paul's final admonition for learning was to **learn by expectation**. He wrote, "Now some are inflated with pride as though I were not coming to you" (1 Cor. 4:18). In today's vernacular, Paul might say, "Some of you don't think daddy's coming home." I seldom liked when my mother said, "Wait till your father gets home." That phrase could mean one of two things. It could mean joy or be prepared for punishment. Are we living in such a way that we really expect that the Father is coming? Paul told the Corinthians, "I am coming to you." Daddies expect great things from their children, because that's what love does; loves expects much. 1 Corinthians 13 explains that if you love someone, you'll be loyal to him or her no matter what the cost. You'll always believe in that person, always expect the best, and always stand your ground in defending him or her. Paul was telling the church, "I expect great things of you." The problem with many children today is that their elders place no expectations upon them; the problem with many churches today is that they believe they have no expectations. Paul told them he expected them to love in power: "I want to see God in you." 1 Corinthians 4:21 says, "What do you want? Should I come to you with a rod or in love and a spirit of gentleness?" Should Paul come with a rod or a rose? Should he come to commend them or to correct them?

One account of a college experiment tells how students were made to wear glasses for ten days, causing everything they viewed through these lenses to be turned upside down. The students had to learn to adapt to an upside-down world. At the conclusion of the ten-day experiment, one of the students said, "It's amazing how soon you get used to living in an upside-down world." Unfortunately, we have become so anesthetized to the craziness that we are "OK" with things being turned upside down today. It is interesting that in the book of Acts, the early church was described with the phrase, "these men have turned the world upside down." I do not presume to correct the Scriptures. But the world was already upside down; these men were the ones who turned the world right-side up. It is so easy for us to get used to a world turned upside-down.

We have a choice. We may choose to live in this upside-down world and learn how to exist. Or we may choose to accept the responsibility of living as a steward of God and saying, "I'm willing to work." We may choose to accept the responsibility of being a spectacle of His glory and to say, "I'm willing to suffer if it is for Him." We may choose to accept the responsibility of being a child of the gospel and to say, "I'm willing to learn; teach me!"

When President Obama muffed his oath of office the media pounced on the incorrect wording administered. News reports confirmed that, later the same evening, the president correctly promised, "I will faithfully execute the office...." One news commentator, upon learning of the event, said, "I really think Americans are not as concerned with what he says as they are with what he does." Likewise, God is not as concerned with what you say as he is with your willingness to accept responsibility for your role: "I will faithfully execute the office of being a believer. I will accept my responsibility to be a steward of yours. I will accept my responsibility to be a spectacle of your glory; I will accept the responsibility of being a child of your gospel."

LESSON 5
STAY CLEAN IN A
FILTHY WORLD

We need to stay clean in a filthy world. Parents of small children know the eagerness in children's faces as they anticipate the opportunity to go outside to play. The immediate admonition as they head out the door is, "But don't get dirty." Don't get dirty? Are there classes in how *not* to get dirty? Corinth was a place described as a seedbed of immorality. It was noted for its hedonistic behavior. I shared with you in the first chapter the city's slogan, "What happens in Corinth stays in Corinth." It was just that kind of city, one filled with filth. Paul advised the Corinthian church, "Be in that filthy and immoral place, but don't get dirty." Today we live in a society where the number of unwed couples living together has tripled in the past ten years. Twenty million sex magazines are sold in the United States every single week and one in eight American adults will be, or already is, an alcoholic.[1] Yet I still believe that God is telling us, "Don't get dirty." In the midst of a world that is filthy, don't get dirty.

How did the city of Corinth address this issue? How do most cities address the issue? They did so with government intervention. Typically problems like these are referred to the court systems. The Greeks were noted for their system of justice. Attempts to legislate were designed to help people understand the difference between right and wrong. The founding of the courtroom system goes back to the ancient Greek culture. The courts were a cheap form of first-century entertainment. Juries were not limited in size and therefore were often very large. People were paid to serve on the jury and so it became a coveted position. It has been recorded that some juries had as many as 6000 members. There was an obvious litigious atmosphere in the first century.

That litigious atmosphere had a great influence upon the early church. I wonder if the same thing may be happening today? We witness two hundred thousand civil suits per year, with over 650,000 lawyers in the United States; twelve million state court cases are pending right now. Courtrooms again have become the chief venue for people's entertainment. Courtroom dramas are among the top television shows in America, in both fiction and reality-based programs.

Did the courtroom endeavors of the first century help the people to stay clean? It didn't work back then and it isn't working for us today. Perhaps we should return to a more biblical approach and the advice of Paul about how to stay clean in a filthy world. In 1 Corinthians 5-6, Paul provided three guidelines to keep the people of the Corinthian church clean.

The Recognition of the Immoral

The first of these guidelines is to **recognize immorality**. Pastor James Carter once told a story about himself as a young pastor with toddlers. His children begged him to get a puppy. Some people are dog people and some people aren't dog people. The people that aren't dog people just cannot stand being around dogs and James Carter was of that breed. Pastor Carter relented, though, to the pressure of his children and they got a puppy. Mistakenly, the family allowed Pastor Carter to name the puppy. What did he name their new puppy who chewed up everything and seemed to make a mess everywhere in the house? He named him "Sin." Imagine the family calling the puppy in their yard, "Here, Sin!" I think that's extremely appropriate. At the time, Pastor Carter was serving a small rural church without air conditioning. One hot summer day, the people threw open the windows of the church and left the doors open so that the whole community could hear the service. Pastor Carter was preaching away when Sin escaped from his pen and began to make his way through the back door of the church. In mid-sentence, the pastor stopped, pointed, and said, "There's Sin in the church!" The amazing thing was that he didn't get an "Amen," an "Oh My," or anything else. He said that not one person responded to the cry. Carter surmised that everyone knew there was sin in the church. But when Paul said, "There is sin in the church," he pointed out what sins and who had committed them. That will grab some people's attention! When someone starts calling out names and naming the sins, I guarantee ears will begin to perk up in the church. Paul informed the people of Corinth, "Here's what's happening."

There is a **depravity in Corinth**. 1 Corinthians 5:1 says, "It is widely reported among you...." Have you noticed that bad news travels fast? People start conversations with, "I don't mean to gossip but...," and then what happens right after that? They gossip! Paul wrote that it had been widely reported that there was "sexual immorality" among the members of the church. The phrase "sexually immorality" is the translation of the Greek word *porneia*, from which we get our English word pornography. The definition of *porneia* in Greek would include any sexual behavior outside the confines of marriage. Thus any sexual activity outside of the marital bond is, by strictest definition, pornographic. Paul says there is *porneia*—immoral sexual behavior going on within the congregation that is not even condoned by the Gentiles. The Gentiles were part of the pagan world, the lost culture. This behavior was so disgusting that pagan people, lost people, did not condone this lifestyle. So what was it? What was the sin? Paul explained that there was a man who was sleeping with his father's wife. Was this incest? It was far more complicated than that, for if it had been his mother, the text would have read "mother." Instead the account reads "his father's wife." This indicates that by all probability the affair was with his step-mother. Most biblical commentators believe that this man was a believer in the Lord Jesus Christ, but that his step-mother was not. The reason for this interpretation is that the man is disciplined in the church for this behavior, but she was not. Leviticus 18:8 says, "You're not to have sex with your father's wife; it will shame you and your father." There is certainly depravity inside the church at Corinth.

The second key to recognizing immorality was noting the **disposition of the church**. Paul noticed the that Corinthians were inflated with pride. The King James Version described them, saying, "you are puffed up, you are proud." Of what were the Corinthians proud? They were proud of being an open-minded people, an accepting people. Their attitude was that they allowed all folks from all walks of life and all kinds of backgrounds to do whatever they wanted to do; it just didn't matter. You can find churches advertising that message in every city in the United States. Whatever you want to do is all right with us. Paul said what the people ought to have been grieving. The word for "grieving" is reminiscent of lamenting over a dead person. What one no longer finds appalling one will eventually find appealing. One should thank God when immorality turns the stomach. One ought to thank God when immorality is disturbing. One ought to be bothered when things that should be bothersome are no longer bothersome. The people in Corinth were puffed up with pride.

The recognition of immorality eventually led to the **discipline of Corinth**. In 1 Corinthians 5:4-5, Paul said that when people meet together they should turn that immoral man "over to Satan." What does that mean? Satan's domain is this world. The Bible says in John 12:31 and John 16:11 that Satan is the prince of this world. God's domain is a spiritual realm. When the scriptures refer to the Kingdom of God, they are referring to the lives of believers. The church is the Kingdom of God. Paul said he wanted the community to turn this man out of the church and over to the world. The world would then destroy him. The Bible declares that there is sin that can happen in the life of a believer that can lead ultimately to death. 1 John 5:16-17 says, "If anyone sees his brother committing a sin that does not bring death, he should ask and God will give life to him—to those who commit sin that doesn't bring death. There is a sin that brings death, I am not saying that he should pray about that." What is the sin that brings about death? There is an obvious line which if crossed, one ceases being a blessing and becomes a burden. If someone lives with openly without confessing habitual sins in his or her life, then there must be a point at which God would say, "It would be better for them to be with me than it would be for them to continue to disgrace me in the world." The "sin unto death" is not losing one's salvation, but having lost one's testimony; they no longer are giving glory to God.

Steve McVey, in his book *The Grace Walk*, wrote, "To continue in sin is not grace, to continue in sin is a disgrace."[2] Dr. H.A. Ironside used to tell a story of a commuter train that had stalled upon the train tracks. Just a few minutes behind the disabled locomotive was a fast-moving freight train that was rapidly closing in. The engineer sent one of his staff out on the tracks and to flag down the fast-approaching freight train to avoid a terrible collision. The engineer calmly informed passengers over the intercom system that the situation was well in hand. The flagman out on the tracks waved a yellow caution flag as the freight train approached. The freight train engineer slowed down the train but did not stop it. Realizing that he was going to crash into the commuter train, the freight engineer jumped from his train and landed safe from harm. But the carnage was absolutely devastating. An investigation of the incident followed and the freight engineer was brought to trial. A review board asked why he did not stop when seeing the flagman. The contrite man answered, "The flagman was waving a yellow flag, which means caution, slow down, and I did slow down. If he had wanted me to stop, why was there not a red flag somewhere on the track?" Dr. Ironside, upon telling this story said, "Oh, the lives eternally wrecked by the 'yellow gospels' in our churches that we are hearing today. The bloodless theories of unregenerate men that sends their hearers to their doom instead of stopping them while they are headed down a road that will go to their eternal doom." [2] God forbid today's church is only raising a yellow flag and saying, "Slow down; take it easy." The church ought to be yelling, "Stop it and stop it right now!" The church must recognize immorality.

The Release of the Immoral

Paul's second step to staying clean in a filthy world was to **release the immoral**. He wrote, "Your boasting is not good, don't you know that a little yeast permeates the whole batch of dough? Clean out the old yeast so that you may be able to have a new batch since you are unleavened. For Christ, our Passover has been sacrificed" (1 Cor. 5:6-7). Leaven in the Jewish culture stood for evil because of how it quickly spread. A similar illustration for our time would be cancer cells in the body. Cancer first must be detected, then it must be diagnosed, and eventually it must be detached in order to restore complete health. Detachment is seldom easy to accomplish. Before the painstaking surgery takes place, there must be acceptance of the condition. Someone has to **respectfully stand** for the truth.

In a Jewish home, before the Passover, family members would go through every single room, sweep every corner, to remove the leaven from the house. Exodus 13:7 says, "Unleavened bread is to be eaten for those seven days. Nothing leavened may be found among you and no yeast may be found among you in all your territory." Today the world hears everything we Christians want to be rid of, everything we stand against. Does the world know what we stand for? The world can enumerate the number of things that the church seems to stand against, but what does the church stand for? The first step of detachment is to make a respectful stand.

The next step of detachment for Paul was to **recapture sincerity**. He wrote, "Therefore, let us observe the feast not with old yeast or with yeast of malice and evil but with the unleavened bread of sincerity and truth" (1 Co. 5:8). The word "sincerity" is actually a compound word that means "judged in the sunlight." When the sun comes out, we are able to see things more clearly. My wife, Glenda, always tells me, "The only good thing about dark gloomy days is that we do not see as clearly the dirt in the house." The sun reveals things. We ought not make judgments according to the standards of pop culture; we ought not judge based upon popular opinion; but we ought to judge all things in the light, in the light of truth.

Detachment involves a respectful stand and a recapturing of sincerity. The final step for Paul was to **renounce support**. This part becomes very difficult for many. 1 Corinthians 5:11 says, "But now, I am writing you, not to associate with any one who bears the name of brother who is sexually immoral or greedy, an idolater or a reviler, a drunkard or a swindler. Do not even eat with such a person." That sounds pretty severe. One needs to understand the word "associate" meant to have business alliance, and the phrase "to eat with" meant to provide for. Therefore, the admonition is to give no support and not encourage this behavior. This does not forbid prayer. But one ought not encourage an individual to continue living in a way that grieves the heart of God. The concept is "tough love." Tough love is never easy. Allowing people to persist in sin makes one, in a legal sense, an accomplice and in counseling terms, an enabler. The church must release these people from its ranks and not promote their continued ungodly activity.

The Redemption of the Immoral

This process is not complete if you don't read the sixth chapter. Paul revealed that the ultimate motive of church discipline was for people to forsake sin and to be redeemed. The goal was to get people to come back or to return to Christ. However, three typical excuses are given for not seeking redemption.

The first was the **ruckus of God's children**. This excuse pointed out that there were hypocrites in the church. 1 Corinthians 6:7-8, "Therefore it is already a total defeat for you that you have law suits against one another; why not rather put up with injustice? Why not rather be cheated? Instead you act unjustly and you cheat and this you do to you own brothers." In the midst of a court system trying to make things right in the world, believers were fighting with one another. Even today, there are no winners when believers fight. There are no winners when churches are torn apart by internal strife.

Remember the Sermon on the Mount? In Matthew 5:39-41, Jesus said,

> I tell you, don't resist an evil doer. On the contrary, if anyone slaps you on your right cheek, turn the other one to him as well. As for the one who wants to sue you and take away your shirt, let him have your coat as well. And if anyone forces you to go one mile, go with him two. Give to the one who asks you, and don't turn away from the one who wants to borrow from you.

The ruckus of God's children has been an excuse for people choosing not to seek redemption. Church people who don't get along with one another harm the cause of Christ.

The second excuse related to the **reality of God's cleansing.** The excuse was "You don't know what I've done." I hear people lament, "Pastor, if you knew the deepest darkest sin in my life...." 1 Corinthians 6:9-11 states,

> Do you not know that the unjust will not inherit God's Kingdom? Do not be deceived; no sexually immoral people, idolaters, adulterers, male prostitutes, homosexuals, thieves, greedy people, drunkards, revilers or swindlers will inherit God's Kingdom. Some of you were like this; but you were washed; you were sanctified; you were justified in the name of the Lord Jesus Christ by the Spirit of our God.

The list given in verse nine is a list of what's commonly called "closet sins." These are activities that people do not want anyone to know about them. Information about these sins may destroy lives. Paul said, "Some of you were involved in those things." The key word is the word "were." That is who they used to be. But their new identity rests in who they were "in Christ." Having given one's life to Christ, they were washed, sanctified, and justified. If we find ourselves in the same position, does that mean that we will never commit another sin or we may never lax again into that same sin pattern from our histories? No, but it means our identity is now given by who we are—forgiven and headed towards an eternity in Heaven. God's cleansing in us has been totally complete. I have had people in my office who would tell me, "Pastor, you don't know what I've done." My response is, "You are right and I do not need to know what you have done. You don't have to confess it to me; I am not your priest. You are a priest with a personal relationship that grants you access straight to the throne of God. God already knows what you have done. And the Bible says, no matter what it is, you can be forgiven." Redemption involves complete cleansing.

There is a third excuse, namely **residence of God's own choosing**. 1 Corinthians 6:16-17 states, "Do you not know that anyone joined to a prostitute is one body with her? For it says, the two will become one flesh. But anyone joined to the Lord is one spirit with Him." This excuse means that one says, in effect, "I've got uncontrollable desires that I have never been able to harness." Many times people using this excuse have been attending counseling or support groups. Some have gone to a Bible study class or sought the persistent advice of peers, friends, and family members. What they have heard repeatedly throughout life was advice to try harder, try this, try more, or try something new. And so they try, and they try, and they try, until they give up. Paul said, "God resides in you." The world is telling you, "You can do it." But the reality is that you can't do it. You really can't. President Obama's campaign slogan that catapulted him to the White House proclaimed, "Yes We Can." Thousands and thousands of people screamed in unison at rallies across America, "Yes We Can." A " Yes We Can" attitude may win you an election, but " Yes We Can" will not keep you clean in a filthy world. Because the reality is this: "No. We can't."

When a toddler comes to a parent and says, "Me do it," what does that mean? It means the parent needs to be patient enough to clean up the mess immediately afterwards. The needed attitude is not "Yes We Can," it is "Yes. God Can." 1 Corinthians 6:20 says, "For you were bought at a price; therefore glorify God in your body." The only hope we have of staying clean in a filthy world is to realize, having given our lives to Christ, the very presence of God in us. And "God can" whenever we can't!

LESSON 6
MAKE MARRIAGE MATTER

Paul recognized the first-century culture was beginning to play havoc with the institution of marriage. The concept of marriage was in deep trouble. Jewish culture had held marriage to a high ideal. In fact, a rabbi would say, "The very altar sheds tears when a man divorces the wife of his youth." Yet, by the time Paul began his ministry, the institution of marriage was in crisis.

Deuteronomy 24:1 says, "When a man has taken a wife and married her and it comes to pass that she finds no favor in his eyes because he has found some uncleanness in her, then let him write her a bill of divorcement and give it to her in hand and send her out of his house" (KJV). Marriages have encountered difficulties since the dawn of time. These difficulties have often led to the dissolution of marriages. Divorce dates back to the Old Testament in the book of Deuteronomy. Divorce was permissible when there was "some uncleanness." What is the definition of "some uncleanness?" Liberal theologians of the first century said, "If she burns the dinner that would be considered some uncleanness. If you ever found her talking to another man, that would be some uncleanness. If you simply found someone you really liked better than her, that would be considered some uncleanness." As in every generation, the liberal interpretations of scripture caused pain and angst. Marriage was in deep trouble when Paul wrote to the first-century Corinthian church.

Marriage today is once again in deep trouble as an institution. In a Zogby/AOL poll from 2007, 44 percent of American adults stated,

"Marriage is not necessary in order to have a committed fulfilling lifelong relationship."[1] Nearly half of Americans say marriage is an outdated institution, a relic of the past. These people view marriage as existing only for the traditionalists. It is merely the church's way of thwarting open-minded lifestyle choices. Forty-four percent of American adults think it is not necessary to get married in order for two people to have a committed, happy life together.

USA Today reports that the U.S. Census estimates have shown for the first time in history there are more unmarried adult households than married adult households in the United States.[2] A special report in *Time* magazine indicates that co-habitation, living together, has risen from 10 percent of couples in 1960 to over 50 percent of couples today.[3] In a Pennsylvania State University study, "The Relationship Between Co-Habitation and Marital Quality and Stability," researchers report that 31 percent of children, (nearly 1 in 3), under the age of eighteen in the United States, live with one parent or no parent at all.[4]

Is the church immune to the societal effects of the dissolution of the concept of marriage? LifeWay Research reports on *Lifeway. com* the top-ten issues facing the church today. The report includes some common items everyone might think would be on such a list: leadership, evangelism, homosexuality, and abortion. Number seven on the list is the issue of marriage.[5] I became curious as to how my own denomination, Baptists, were faring as marriage entered a freefall. After all, we, as Baptists, have been noted as traditionalists, "people of the book." Barna Research Group reports that of all the mainline denominations—Presbyterians, Methodists, Pentecostals, Episcopalians, Lutherans, and Baptists—Baptists have the highest divorce rate. (29 percent, 4 percent higher than the average)[6]

Business Week magazine reports that the Hallmark Card Company has reduced its production of Silver Anniversary cards. When a company vice-president was asked to comment, the reply was "People are just not staying married that long anymore."[7] Michael McManus, president of an organization known as "Marriage Savers" (a ministry to rescue marriages), says "Churches aren't really very marriage minded, they are more wedding minded. They are equipped to help couples have weddings but they do very little to help couples build a marriage."[8] If we are going to "be the church," and not just do church or play church, we will need to start making marriage matter.

Remember that 1 Corinthians is actually a letter written as a reply. Paul wrote to the Corinthians specifically responding to questions they had asked him. Thus, 1 Corinthians 7 does not contain a complete theology of marriage; it is actually an advice column written in response to specific questions the Corinthians had asked Paul about marriage. You can divide this advice into three categories. Paul had **advice for united households; advice for divided households** and **advice for single households**.

Advice For United Households

The first group that Paul addressed in 1 Corinthians 7 is Christians who were married to other Christians. There is one apparent question that Paul wanted to answer, "Is celibacy more spiritual than getting married?" Is it more spiritual to be married or remain unmarried?" Paul began his comments on marriage by **setting the standard**. What should be the standard by which we should evaluate marriage?

Recall in 1 Corinthians 6:18, he advised to "flee from sexual immorality." In some other translations, the term used is "fornication." The Greek word is *porneia*. This is the root of the English word pornography; it literally means any sexual relationship outside of the confines of marriage. These do not fulfill God's intended purpose. Paul explained two ways that one could avoid *porneia*. One could choose the celibacy route or one could choose the marriage route. Which of those was superior? There was a strong group in the first century, known as the Gnostics, who were making waves in the church. The Gnostics believed the body was evil and only the spirit was good. This fundamental belief influenced their interpretation of scripture. One possible interpretation rendered by the Gnostics would be that since the body was evil and everything about it was evil, just let the body do whatever it wants, and the spirit will be saved. Let the body fulfill its every fleshly desire. The other interpretation might be, since the body was evil, it needs to be punished, completely denying anything that the body is interested in and desires. This debate had become so public that a widespread inclination had even infiltrated the church to say that any sexual relationship could be a sin. Therefore, celibacy was lifted up as the better choice, just in case.

It is amazing how an idea can become authoritative based upon someone's opinion rather than upon scripture. In the first church I served as pastor, there was a congregant who would come up with the most outlandish sayings. I would ask him, "Where did you learn that?" His most common response was, "Well, it is in the Bible or Grandma said it. I forget which." For him the two were equally authoritative. One needs to determine if one is making decisions based upon scripture or merely what one has heard from others in life.

From the very beginning, as recorded in Genesis 2:18, God said, "It is not good that man should be alone, I will make him a helpmate for him." The Bible, and not an opinion poll, is our standard. It doesn't matter what Oprah says; it doesn't matter what the Kinsey report says; it doesn't matter what popular opinion polls say. If the Bible is our standard, then the most important question asks, "What does the Bible have to say about it?" God intended for us to be in relationships and he is the one setting the standards.

The second area of advice to united households was the **sacredness of sex**. 1 Corinthians 7:3-5 says,

> A husband should fulfill his marital duty to his wife and likewise a wife to her husband. A wife does not have authority over her own body but her husband does. Equally, a husband does not have authority over his own body, but his wife does. Do not deprive one another except when you agree for a time to devote yourself to prayer. Then come together again; otherwise, Satan may tempt you.

The Bible indicates that sexual relations were intended for marriage. God created men and women and made them sexual beings.

In Matthew 19:6, Jesus said," So they are no longer two but one flesh. Therefore what God has joined together, man must not separate." The term "deprive" in 1 Corinthians 7:5 ("defraud" in some translations) comes from a Greek word meaning to rob or to cheat. Sexual love is a tool for building up a relationship and not a weapon for fighting. Yet for many, the bedroom has become a battlefield in their family lives.

A friend and Christian counselor once said, "There are no sexual problems in marriages, only personality problems that tend to have sexual relations as their symptoms." As Paul wrote in 1 Corinthians 7:5, "...otherwise, Satan may tempt you." The Devil knows homes in which the bedroom has become a battlefield. Satan is aware of marriages where the improper expression of sexual relations is a tremendous temptation. You may recall Jesus' warning in his conversation with Simon Peter. The night Jesus was betrayed, He said, "Tonight Peter, Satan desires to have you that he may sift you like wheat." In other words, Satan seeks the most vulnerable spot in one's life; there is where he will attack. Satan is still sifting today. He is still finding the vulnerable spots in people's lives and attacking at full force.

Understanding God's intentions brings about the greatest satisfaction in a person's relational life. The Family Research Council of Washington, D.C., has found that people who are most likely to report a high degree of satisfaction with their current sex life are married people who strongly believe that sex outside of marriage is wrong. This group's satisfaction rate is 72 percent, 31 percent higher than unmarried non-traditionalist thinkers, and 13 percent higher than married non-traditionalist thinkers.[9] Let that statistic sink in for a while. The people most satisfied with their sex lives are those who believe that sex is reserved for marriage and who think sex outside of marriage is wrong. Further, the most satisfied among that satisfied group are those who attend church regularly. If there is a problem in the bedroom, it may stem from a faulty premise about sexual satisfaction.

Paul gave a third word of advice to united households concerning the **sin of separation**. The Christian life had brought such radical changes to the early first-century believers that the Corinthians wanted to know, "Do we need to stay married?" Marriage was viewed by some as a hindrance to total pursuit of the cause of Christ. 1 Corinthians 7:8-9 says," I say to the unmarried and the widows, it is good for them that they remain as I am. But if they do not have self-control, they should marry for it is better to marry than to burn with desire." That has always been a favorite quote from scripture,

"…better to marry than to burn…." This does not state the rationale for marriage. The word "burn" means to be inflamed with passionate desire. Some think, "Since God made me that way, why fight it?" The next verse says, "I command the married, not I but the Lord, a wife is not to leave her husband. But if she does leave, she must remain unmarried or be reconciled to her husband and a husband is not to leave his wife" (1 Cor. 7:10). The advice of Paul was this: do everything humanly possible to preserve the marital bond.

Jesus addressed this issue in his Sermon on the Mount. Matthew 5:32 states, "I tell you, everyone who divorces his wife, except for a case of sexual immorality, causes her to commit adultery and whoever marries a divorced woman commits adultery." When Paul gave advice to Christians who were married to other Christians, he pointed out the standard has been set; the standard was the word of God, and not the opinions of people. God intends for a man and a woman to celebrate their sexual relationships within inside the marital bond. It is a sin to seek separation from marriage, even if it is to try to pursue God with more fervor.

Advice for Divided Households

Paul's second response was **advice to the divided household**. This was not addressed merely to couples who were separated; it referred precisely to Christians married to non-Christians, to believers married to non-believers. Some of the Corinthians were saved after they had been married and so they wanted to know what they ought to do about their marriages. How should they respond faithfully? The first question on the hearts of many of these people was "May we have permission to divorce?" There were two circumstances Paul addressed specifically. First was the situation in which an unbelieving spouse was willing to stay in the relationship. Paul said to that group, "Stay." Marriage was a physical relationship and should only be broken by a physical cause—adultery or death. The apostle Peter gave advice to women in the first century who had unbelieving husbands, as 1 Peter 3:1-4 says,

> Wives, in the same way, submit yourselves to your own
> husbands so that even if some disobey the Christian

message, they may be won over without a message by the way their wives live, when they observe your pure, reverent lives. Your beauty should not consist of outward things like elaborate hair styles and the wearing of gold ornaments or fine clothes; instead it should consist of the hidden person of the heart with the imperishable quality of a gentle and quiet spirit which is very valuable in God's eyes.

The first circumstance Paul addressed was unbelievers who were willing to stay in the relationship.

What if they left? 1 Corinthians 7:15 says, "But if the unbeliever leaves, let him leave. A brother or a sister is not bound in such cases, God has called you to peace." It is very important to note, Paul did *not* say that when the unbeliever leaves, the remaining spouse should seek a divorce and cut off the relationship. In some instances, love must be tough to stand for what is right. The principle is expressed in the next verse. "For you, wife, how do you know whether you will save your husband; or you husband, how do you know whether you will save your wife" (1 Cor. 7:16)? The Christian influence that a believer brings to a relationship may be the only Christian influence that the spouse will ever experience. Therefore, make every effort to make the relationship work. The advice to divided households seeking permission to divorce is that permission is denied. Work it out.

The second area of advice for divided households was to provide a **principle in direction**. This section, 1 Corinthians 7:17-24, is often times referred to as a parenthetical paragraph because it does not appear to go with the rest of the advice concerning marital relationships. Some Bible teachers accuse Paul of a little rabbit-chasing binge here. Perhaps he had thought of something that didn't apply to the specific subject at hand but then returned to the marriage matter later. I. however, believe these verses relate to the subject of marriage and lie very much at the heart of his teaching. 1 Corinthians 7:17 says, "However, each one must live his life in the situation the Lord assigned when God called him." Then in 1 Corinthians 7:20, Paul wrote, "Each person should remain in the life situation in which he was called." A little later, in 1 Corinthians 7:24, he added, "Brothers, each person should remain with God in whatever situation he was called." Three times in this one paragraph Paul said to stay put in the place where God has put one.

Recently our church went through the study, *Lord Change My Attitude*, by James MacDonald.[9] The first negative trait dealt with in the study is the attitude of complaining. How many times in our lives do we find ourselves complaining about the situation in which we find ourselves? People complain about their job, marriage, financial situation, friends, church, and the list can go on and on and on. Could it be that God has placed me in this specific situation at this specific time for a specific purpose? Yet many are saying, "I don't care!" One may be in a storm for a reason, a purpose. The storms in relationships can be opportunities for God to do wonderfully redemptive work that could only be accomplished through the hardship of the situation. Therefore, Paul said, "Stay put."

Advice for the Single Household

Paul concludes this chapter with some **advice for the single household**. Until recently, most young people chose marriage. That traditional choice is rapidly changing. Several factors have led to the downward spiral of marriage. Many young people delay marriage in order to further their education. We are the most educated society in history. Many remain single in order to meet job demands and advance careers, to be first in line for company promotions. And also, there are more divorced and widowed people in the United States than ever before. These three factors bolstered the number of single people so much that they now outnumber married people in this country.

Paul gave some direct, yet kind advice to singles. His first word to singles was, "You need to **get ready**. Consider the circumstances in which we now live." In 1 Corinthians 7:29, he wrote, "I say this, brothers, the time is limited." Some translations say the time is "short." Some singles may think the "window of time" for marriage has passed them by. The phrase "time is limited" refers to a coming crisis. Paul had said in 1 Corinthians 6:26, "Therefore, I consider this to be good because of the present distress." To what crisis was Paul referring? He was admonishing the upside-down church in Corinth; the community's situation would affect whether or not some people would get married. Paul recognized that sometimes a crisis must be faced before one is free to decide to marry.

Global crises have affected marrying patterns throughout history. Soldiers came back from World War II amid a greatly celebrative atmosphere throughout our country. An economic boom followed the end of the war. As a result, more babies were born than ever before in our history. I am a product of what was referred to as the "Baby Boom." Then in the 1960s and into the early 1970s, the Cold War took place. People became cautious and didn't want to bring children into a world haunted by nuclear threat. Birth rates became the lowest they had been in over two centuries. "Consider the circumstances" seems to be good advice.

In the first meeting of my pre-marital counseling sessions with each engaged couple, I have a section I refer to as "Let's Talk." Let's talk about your situation. Let's talk about finances; let's talk about your backgrounds; and let's talk about what is going to affect you in your relationship. Consider the circumstance and get ready for marriage.

In this country the average age of a groom has risen to twenty-eight years and the average age of a bride has risen to twenty-six years for first time marriages In the 1960s a groom was twenty-three and a bride was twenty.[10] Couples are waiting longer and are heeding the advice, "Get ready, and consider the circumstances."

Paul's next word to singles was **get responsible**. Be willing to divide your energy. A key word in 1 Corinthians 7:32-35 is "concern." This word literally means to be torn in two different directions. That is a poignant description of married life. Every married person has dealt with feeling divided or being torn in different directions. The married person should never forget that marriage is a responsibility. I do not have only myself to think about anymore; I must consider my spouse and my family. In Luke 14:26, Jesus said, "If anyone comes to me and does not hate his own father and mother; wife and children, brothers and sisters, yes and even his own life, he cannot be my disciple." That is a passage you do not very often hear in preaching. Jesus was saying that feeling the pull of divided directions brings one to the point of deciding that Christ is first! I advise all couples getting married to take on the responsibility of no longer living for oneself. You are a part of a team.

The National Survey of Families and Households says that among couples who are living together, who co-habit before marriage, half break up before getting married. Of those who do get married, 80 percent of them will divorce.[11] Why? Because they have not made the commitment on the front end, they have no relationship as a team. The only responsibility in these relationships is responsibility for self.

Paul's third word to single households was to **get reasonable**. Don't marry just to get married. Have you ever noticed that weddings come in bunches? Who said that marriage has to take place between the ages of twenty and twenty-seven? I found a business sign that read, "Guns and Wedding Gowns Sold Here; we are a one-stop-shop kind of place." 1 Corinthians 7:36 is addressed to those who past the marrying age (or in the King James Version, the "flower of her age"). I wrote in the margin of my Bible, "What age is that?" Paul never identified it. If you believe you are culturally past the marrying age, do not marry just to be married. A pastor friend of mine, early in my ministry, said it was better to live in single loneliness than it is to live in married *"cussedness."* Marriage is far too great a thing for you to enter into lightly. Get reasonable.

The fourth and final word to singles was **get real.** In 1 Corinthians 7:39-40, Paul closed this entire passage out by reminding them that marriage was a lifetime commitment. The Bible says in Malachi 2:16 that "God hates divorce." It does not say that God hates divorced people, but God hates what divorce does to children. He hates what divorce does to homes; he hates what divorce does to churches; and he hates what divorce does to his kingdom's purposes. Paul admonished people to build relationships that would last. Paul concluded with the thought that if a woman were looking for a husband, she could look for anyone she wanted. 1 Corinthians 7:39 offers the qualifying phrase, "only in the Lord." For us, the most important thing is to recognize whom God wants for me, whom God intends for me.

Charles Swindoll wrote *The Quest for Character* several years ago. In it, he quotes a sociologist and historian by the name of Carl Zimmerman. In 1947 Zimmerman said, "Marriage is the bedrock of every civilization that has ever been known to man." Zimmerman noted that there were eight specific patterns of domestic behavior typical of a downward spiral in every culture. The beginning comes when marriage loses its sacredness.

> It is frequently broken by divorce and the traditional meaning of the marriage ceremony is lost. Feminist movements abound and there is an increased public disrespect for parents and authority in general. An acceleration of juvenile delinquency; promiscuity and rebellion occurs. There is a refusal of people with traditional marriages to accept family responsibilities. A growing desire for and acceptance of adultery is evident and there is an increasing interest in and spread of sexual perversions and sexually related crimes.[12]

Zimmerman wrote that in 1947, but it sounds rather current. When marriage loses its sacredness, society crumbles.

Paul was saying to the first-century church, when marriage loses its sacredness, when marriage doesn't matter anymore, society crumbles. He told those with united households to follow the standard of God's holy word, to realize that God had put them together, to understand that the sacredness of a sexual relationship abides within the confines of marriage, and to know it is a sin to think about separating. To those living in divided households where a believer is married to an unbeliever, Paul said that permission to divorce was denied. He exhorted them to do everything they could to stay the course and to weather the storm. And his advice to single households was to get ready, get responsible, get reasonable, and get real because marriage is a lifetime commitment. We are called to make marriage matter because we want to" be the church" and not just do church.

LESSON 7
MAKE GODLY
DECISIONS IN
GRAY AREAS

ow do you make godly decisions in the gray areas of life? I think almost everyone agrees that decisiveness is considered a mark of leadership. Decisive people tend to rise to the top. They tend to be the achievers in the business world, the scholars of the academic world, the top in every known field because of their capacity for decisive action.

Peter Drucker, the "Father of Business Management" said, "Whenever you see a successful business, someone once made a courageous decision."[1] Think back to the great business success stories. Sam Walton decided that a department store would work in a small town, and if it would work in one small town it would work in every small town across this country. Thus was born a creative and successful business decision.

Steve Jobs was putting together computers in his garage in California and thought "every home ought to have one of these." He made a courageous and successful business decision. Where is the next generation of courageous entrepreneurs? Who is going to help us get beyond the financial quagmire that we find ourselves in as a nation? I read recently about a young man with great promise hired right out of college by a company with high expectations for their new recruit. He was promoted rapidly through the company. Soon he found himself in a position with the company where he did not know what to do. The young executive approached one of the old sages in the company and asked how best to perform his new task. The tenured employee advised him, "Two words: right decisions." The rising star lamented, "But I need to know how to make right decisions." The senior exec quipped, "One word: experience." The frustrated young seeker asked, "How do I get experience?" The patient advisor looked him in the eye and said, "Wrong decisions."

There has to be another way to be able to make right decision without always having to learn form the experience of making wrong decisions. I did a Google search, typing "decision making" and hitting enter. The number-one site returned was entitled "The Society for Judgment and Decision Making." On the site's front page is an explanation of the organization. "The Society for Judgment and Decision Making is an interdisciplinary academic organization dedicated to the study of normative descriptive and prescriptive theories of decisions. Its members include psychologists, economists, organizational researchers, decision analysts and other decision researchers." If anybody knows how to make good decisions, these people ought to know. I navigated through this information and found a link to the society's "article of the month." What was the article of the month on the Society for Judgment and Decision Making Web site? "Does Anyone Know What's Going on Out There?"[2]

People are looking for decision-makers today. Just as world leaders are decision-makers, leaders in the church are decision-makers. John Maxwell is considered a church leadership guru, author of *21 Irrefutable Laws of Leadership*. In his book, Maxwell states, "Successful leaders have the courage to take action rather than to hesitate."[3] So, we are torn between not knowing what to do and knowing that good leadership is to take action. How do you reconcile this dilemma? This sounds like an episode of Oprah. Actually, it was an episode of Oprah. There is not a subject that this pop icon has not attempted to shed light or her slant on. Oprah says, "You never have to do anything. If you don't know what to do, do nothing." Tell that to a family who's deciding whether to choose chemotherapy for their terminally ill relative after debating between quantity and quality of life. Tell that to the person who is trying to decide whether or not to expose a friend's addiction problem after mentally debating between confidentiality or genuinely caring about the welfare of the loved friend. How do I make those types of decisions when doing nothing is not an option?

President Theodore Roosevelt once said, "In any moment of decision, the best thing to do is the right thing, the next best thing to do is the wrong thing and the worst thing to do is nothing."[4] So if the best thing to do is the right thing, how do you know the right thing to do? Since I used an Oprah quotation, how about a word from Dr. Phil? Dr. Phil says, "Sometimes you make the right decision and sometimes you make the decision right." The apostle Paul gave his advice to the Corinthians, "When you don't know the right thing to do, know the right way to decide."

The Reasoning of Important Decisions

In most translations, 1 Corinthians 8 begins with the words "now about." This is a phrase from a formula that indicates Paul was specifically addressing a question the Corinthians had raised. At the very outset of this chapter Paul pointed to the **reasoning of important decision-making**. The problem was that there were two sources of meat in the first century. The first source was the regular market place, but the market price had escalated beyond most people's means. Many of us can relate to that. If you have gone to the grocery store lately, you may have seen the market price of meat skyrocket. But in Paul's day there was a second source of meat. One could go to the local temples and secure the meat that had been offered to the idols. Sacrifices would only require a portion of the animal, oftentimes the hindquarters. Therefore, the rest of the meat would be sold. People could find a bargain at the local temple. The question this raised among believers was whether Christians should buy meat that has been offered to an idol. Also, should a Christian even attend a banquet in which the meat being served had been offered to an idol? Paul indicated in his response to this perplexing issue that there was no scriptural imperative defining what to do in this circumstance. So Paul alluded to three guiding principles for dealing with decisions of this nature.

The first guiding principle was **a love connection**. Meat that was offered to idols did not hold any significance to Christians because they did not believe in the idols. They realized that idols were mere representations of a god, and not the true God. This is why in 1 Corinthians 8:1 many translations say, "We all have knowledge" in quotation marks. Paul was quoting what he has heard directly from the Corinthians, "We all know that idols are not real." Knowledge is good to have but one needs to be careful. Any time one engages in self-defense or makes an argument by saying, "I know," one is being prideful. Knowledge is not the final determining factor in making a decision. If knowledge is not the final determining factor, what is? Paul said love is. Paul also wrote in Ephesians 4:15, "Speak the truth in love." Knowing the facts is not the driving determinant of godly decision-making, for love is the key.

1 Corinthians 13 is considered the great love chapter. 1 Corinthians 13:2 says, "If I have the gift of prophesy and understand all mysteries and all knowledge and if I have all faith so that I could move mountains but do not have love, I am nothing." No matter how much you know, no matter how much you think you have your facts straight, no matter how much you reason, the determining factor is love. So for us the first principle in godly decision-making is to have a love connection.

Paul's second principle was a **level conscience**. 1 Corinthians 8:7 says, "However, not everyone has this knowledge. In fact some have been so used to idolatry up until now that when they eat food offered to an idol, their conscience, being weak, is defiled." Now the word "conscience" translates a Greek compound word meaning "know-with." The conscience is that which confirms knowledge. This word, appearing thirty-two times in the New Testament, means the internal "court" that takes place inside one when seeking to determine the difference between right and wrong. The conscience is like a tool—the level. If you have ever used a level, you know that when the bubble settles in the middle, then your work is straight, that it is correct. So when someone calls you "level-headed" it means you make good decisions. The Bible says in 1 Timothy 1:5, "Now the goal of our instruction is love from a pure heart; a good conscience and a sincere faith." When love is our motivation, the Bible declares that we will have a good conscience. The level is correct.

A second type of conscience described in this text is a **defiled conscience**. People have one of two kinds of conscience, a good conscience or a defiled conscience. The word "defiled" literally means messed up. Imagine someone breaks into your house, gets into your toolbox tonight, tampering with your level and somehow change its calibration so that everything you measure from now on is incorrect. The next time you go to build something, thinking that it is straight and perpendicular, you find your project turns out crooked and pitched because your level is off. Paul basically said one could not make one's work straight and true if the level were incorrect. Titus 1:15 says, "To the pure everything is pure, but to those who are defiled and unbelieving, nothing is pure; in fact both their mind and their conscience are defiled." In those part of life that are not black and white and we don't have a clear scriptural commandment, we must depend upon a conscience; our conscience must be surrendered to God.

Paul's third principle of godly reasoning was to have a **legitimate care**. 1 Corinthians 8:9 says, "But be careful that this right of yours in no way becomes a stumbling block to the weak." Whatever a Christian does, even if it does not hurt him, it must not hurt anyone else. Paul said the primary motivation in making decisions had to be that one legitimately cared about other people. You care enough to ask an individual how a situation will affect him or her. Let me give you a personal example of this principle. I realize that for some people it is very difficult to draw a totally biblical argument for abstinence from consumption of alcohol. Congregants have challenged me, "Pastor, I do not see a biblical forbiddance of alcohol, therefore I sense a freedom in this area of my life." I have honestly searched the scriptures and found the Bible speaks about wine as a "mocker" and strong drink as a "brawler." The Bible is clear about the abuse of alcohol, but to make a decision about abstinence of alcohol, you have to go beyond that scriptural argument. For my entire adult life I have made the decision I would abstain from alcohol. And I have done so with these passages from the Bible in mind. People ask me, "Pastor, how did you come to that conclusion?" I came to that conclusion because I didn't want any parents to ever hear from their teenager on prom night, "Yeah, I did drink, Mom and Dad, but you know I saw the Pastor out buying a beer, so I figured it was alright." I do not want the spouse of a person with alcoholism to ever hear from that person, "We saw the pastor out last week with a glass of wine on his table at the restaurant." So I made the decision out of love for a weaker brother. Does my decision encourage or does it enrage a weaker believer?

The Rights of Individual Decisions

How do you make godly decisions in the gray areas of life? Paul provided sound reasoning for making important decisions. Then in 1 Corinthians 9 he shared the **rights of an individual decision**. Am I supposed to always think about others? What about me, what about personal decisions that I may need to make? What about my rights? Chapter 9 is actually Paul's personal testimony about how he came to grips with surrendering the rights of decision-making. First, Paul said, one has a **right to receive**. 1 Corinthians 9:7 says, "Who ever goes to war at his own expense? Who plants a vineyard and does not eat its fruit? Or who shepherds a flock and does not drink the milk from the flock?" I have a right to receive the natural products of my labor. A soldier can say he receives support from the country because he defends the country. A farmer can say she receives the fruit of the land because she is the one who tills the land. A shepherd can say he gets milk and meat from the flock because he is the keeper of the flock. By the way, all three of these illustrations describe of the work of a pastor: a soldier battling Satan and protecting the church; a farmer sowing seed and tending the field; a shepherd leading and feeding the sheep. Paul made the argument as a minister of the gospel; I have a right to receive the natural fruits of my labor.

Paul's second argument was that one had a **right to refuse**. 1 Corinthians 9:15 says, "But I have used none of these rights, and I have not written this to make it happen that way for me. For it would be better for me to do than for anyone to deprive me of my boast." It would be better for Paul to refuse his rights than to deprive him of his boasting. Of what was Paul boasting? Paul said of himself, "I boast in nothing but boasting in the Lord. I have a right to refuse so that I can give all the attention to the Lord." The first century wasn't much different from the twenty-first century in that many in the unsaved world were convinced that preaching was little more than religious racketeering. It was viewed as nothing more than a sacred con game. Paul said he had a right to refuse so that the message would not be diluted, so it would not be watered down; so all the attention would be given to his savior, Jesus Christ.

Paul said he had a right to receive, a right to refuse and then a **right to reform**. 1 Corinthians 9:22-23 states, "To the weak I became weak in order to win the weak. I have become all things to all people so that I might by all means save some. Now I do all this because of the gospel that I may become a partner in its benefits." Was Paul a chameleon; was he inconsistent? Paul's description sounds to us like a weather vane turning with the winds of change. The weather vane appears to be inconsistent. One day it is pointing north, one day to the south, then to the east on another day, and on yet another day to the west. In reality the weather vane is not inconsistent; it is consistent with the wind. Paul was not inconsistent, but was consistent with the wind of leadership of God's Spirit. You could paraphrase this passage by saying, "I became a Colts fan that I might win a football junkie; I became a brick mason that I might win a construction worker; I became a philosopher that I might win a college professor." The key is that one does this to "save" some. We have the right to reform if the result brings people to the Lord Jesus Christ.

Paul then proceeded in this personal illustration, saying he had a **right to reward**: "Do you not know that the runners in a stadium all race but only one receives the prize? Run in such a way that you may win" (1 Cor. 9:24) And then he wrote, "Instead I discipline my body and bring it under strict control so that after preaching to others, I myself will not be disqualified" (1 Cor. 9:27) Paul said he had a right to reward because he had not been disqualified. Paul said "I want to win" but maintained he wanted to win by not being disqualified. The word "disqualified" literally means "not able to stand the test."

Some avid football fans enter into spirited debate about the merits of the game's instant replay. Should we have it? Should we not have it? Does it delay the game? One thing is certain; the instant replay has people looking closely at the details of an official's judgment call. Whether someone was in or out, whether the player made the catch or didn't make the catch. Sometimes the action is delayed while a referee drapes his head with a cape and watches the replay on a monitor. Everyone catching the broadcast sees the play over and over and over again. Is it foot in or is it out? Did he catch the ball or did he not catch it? The Bible says God knows those who are in and those who are out.

In John 14:6, the apostle shares Jesus' saying, "I am the way, the truth and the life; no man comes to the Father except through me." We can debate it back and forth among ourselves. We can say we think he's in or she's in, we think he's out or she's out. But the truth is God knows who is qualified and who is disqualified. Paul said he had a right to reward because he had not been disqualified. With Paul, we can say, "I'm in. I've given my life to Christ."

The Results of Improper Decisions

In 1 Corinthians 10, Paul's attention turns to the **results of some improper decisions**. We might wonder, whether one does so ignorantly or deliberately, what if one chooses to do the wrong thing? And in this section, Paul gave three warnings. First Paul said there is a danger of **falling into sin**. As the chapter unfolds, it retells the story of the deliverance of the children of Israel from Egypt. Paul reminded the Corinthians that their ancestors once followed a cloud by day and a pillar of fire by night, passing through the Red Sea and enjoying deliverance from the Egyptian army. They ate manna in the wilderness when they were out of food, yet they complained. God rained down bread from heaven and yet they said, "But we don't have any water!" So Moses struck a rock and water poured forth from it. The people were blessed and blessed and blessed and blessed! 1 Corinthians 10:5 says, "But God was not pleased with most of them for they were struck down in the desert." The phrase "struck down" is the translation of the Greek word at the root of our word "catastrophe." In the paragraph that follows, Paul reminded them of the great catastrophe of a people so blessed by God. In 1 Corinthians 10:7-10, Paul wrote that they turned to idolatry, then to sexual immorality, then to tempting and testing God's patience, and finally to complaining to one another. Among the sins on this list—idolatry, immorality, tempting and testing God, and complaining—the pinnacle of that list would be complaining.

In James MacDonald's wonderful devotional study, *Lord, Change My Attitude*, the first attitude dealt with complaining. One day I was reading the lesson during my morning quiet time in my home office.

When I completed the lesson and emerged from the office, my wife, Glenda, asked me about my study. Being a LifeWay trustee, I am always critiquing Bible study materials. So I responded, "I would have written it a little differently. The material covered so many Scripture texts today in an attempt to arrive at the major point. I believe I would have centered on one Scripture passage." Glenda looked at me with some disgust and said, "Are you complaining about your lesson about not complaining?" I painfully admitted, "Yes I am.... I think I need to go back into my quiet time for a while longer."

The children of Israel were blessed and blessed and blessed and how did they respond to it? They complained. People tell me all the time, "Pastor, I don't mean to complain but...." Then what do they do? Complain!

The second danger is that of having **fellowship with sin**. Chapter 10:14 reads, "Therefore, my dear friends, flee from idolatry." The word "flee" means to run away from. This word appears in the present tense in the Greek, implying continuing action. So to "flee" means to run away and not to stop running away. Run and keep on running. James 4:7 says, "Therefore, submit to God. But resist the Devil, and he will flee from you." Later in 1 Corinthians 10: 21-22, the text says, "You cannot drink the cup of the Lord and the cup of demons. You cannot share in the Lord's Table and the table of demons. Or are we are provoking the Lord to jealously? Are we stronger than He is?" One cannot sit at the table of Jesus and sit at the table of demons. You have to make a decision. Those who play with matches will get burned.

The final result for bad decisions is the danger of **fostering other's sin**. 1 Corinthians 10:23-24 states, "Everything is permissible but not everything is helpful. Everything is permissible but not everything builds up. No one should seek his own good but the good of the other person." Why? The answer appears in 1 Corinthians 10:32033: "Give no offense to the Jews or to the Greeks or to the church of God, just as I also try to please all people in all things, not seeking my own profit, but the profit of many, that they may be saved." The key component in decision-making is one word—others. And it is with one primary purpose—salvation. Like it or not, the world observes what the church's actions. In the gray areas of life, in which

73

one does not know absolutes but depends upon principles that God has revealed to one's heart, one question arises: What is the decision and how does one make it?

I once read a story about a guy who approached every decision, no matter how big or small it was, by taking a coin from his pocket and flipping it. Heads, do this; tails, do that. He went to a fast food restaurant—heads for the burger and tails for the chicken sandwich, He flipped the coin and then ordered. If he was getting dressed in the morning, he flipped the coin—heads for the blue jeans and tails for the khakis. Living his life ruled by chance was driving his friends crazy. Finally, one of his friends intervened and challenged him. The coin-flipping man responded to his critic, "Rather than me flip the coin, I'll let you flip the coin." The friend asked, "How does that change anything?" The confused friend received the coin and upon examination learned that the coin was heads on both sides. What people looked at as making decisions by chance was actually making a decision based upon his conscience, what he thought was the right thing to do at the time. Oprah can say, "Do nothing. If you don't know what to do, just do nothing." But Paul said not to make decisions a matter of fate, make them a matter of faith. Do not leave a decision up to chance; make it a matter of your conscience. Make sure your conscience is level by surrendering totally to God.

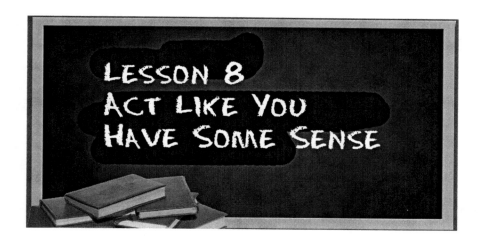

LESSON 8
ACT LIKE YOU
HAVE SOME SENSE

Everyone has seen videos on television or YouTube where people attempt outlandish stunts, only to end up visiting an emergency room and becoming the punch line in someone's story. I recently watched a video of a man pushing his car on a snow-covered road till it topped a hill, gained momentum coming down the other side. Down the road the man chased his driverless vehicle until it crashed into a neighbor's home. The common advice to offer these disaster seekers is "Act like you have some sense."

Many people seem to have lost the ability for simple reasoning today. This plight effects even the upper extremes of our society. A key example is the government bailout of the American auto industry. The big three automakers' CEO's went before Congress and asked for billions of dollars in order to aid their ailing industry. On their first occasion to testify before Congress, these begging executives arrived in Washington, D.C., aboard three separate private jets. The senators asked whether, at least, they could not have settled for first class commercial flights or shared a private jet and "jet pooled" their way to Washington. This is a far cry from just a couple of decades ago. Sam Walton, deceased CEO of Wal-Mart, was at one time the richest man in the United States. He drove a 1988 Ford pick-up truck until the day of his death in 1994. He was once quoted as saying, "If American management is going to say to their workers that we're all in this together, then they're going to have to stop the foolishness of paying themselves three to four million dollar bonuses every year; riding around in limos and corporate jets like they are so much better than everybody else."[1] Many people would characterize the automakers' behavior as foolishness.

The Bible uses the words "fool, folly, or foolishness" 360 times, almost one time for every day of the year. People who do not possess wisdom are referred to as "fools" in the Bible. Their behavior is called "folly" and the result of their behavior is called "foolishness." Proverbs 1:7 says, "The fear of the Lord is the beginning of wisdom." The *Holman Bible Dictionary* defines a fool as someone who is indifferent to God. Psalm 14:1 says, "The fool says in his heart God does not exist. They are corrupt; their actions are revolting. There is no one who does good."

It is important to note that the fool says "in his heart," there is no God. A fool may not profess to be an atheist, but he or she practices atheism. The fool is not necessarily the person who "says" there is no God. The fool is someone who "acts" as if there is no God, whose life choices indicate disbelief in an Almighty who is in control of all things.

Charles R. Swindoll wrote a book entitled *Living on the Ragged Edge*. I love that title, but also the subtitle, *Finding Joy in a World Gone Mad*. In this book, he wrote,

> No amount of arguing, persuading, pleading, threatening or even throwing profanity back at the fool will change him or her. Bargaining won't work either. Logic will break down; tears will not be effective. Strong discipline won't even work once the fool gets old enough. Because what fools do best is act foolish.[2]

Proverbs 19:3 says, "A man's own foolishness leads him astray, yet his heart rages against the Lord." Paul instructed the early church to act differently from the foolishness of the world. Christians need to act from a different motivation. You need to act like you have some sense.

The Example of Intervention

In 1 Corinthians 11, Paul noted three examples of wise choices to be made. The first was an **example of intervention**. The example of intervention is to dress like one has some sense. Remember, Paul wrote in response to some specific questions that have been asked of him by the Corinthians. One of those questions obviously was about appropriate attire, about dressing correctly.

Paul's advice began by noting the Corinthians' **dishonorable actions** in 1 Corinthians 10:1-5. "I want you to know that Christ is the head of every man and the man is the head of the woman and God is the head of Christ" (1 Cor. 10:3). This passage often will lead people into trouble as they try to ascertain its meaning and understand its application. Headship issues are certainly a part of Scripture. I want to be very clear that headship never implies inferiority. The head of Christ is God. Is Christ or God the inferior in this relationship? Headship has nothing to do with who is superior or who is inferior. In Philippians 2:6-7, the Bible speaks of Christ who, "existing in the form of God did not consider it equality with God as something to be used for his own advantage. Instead he emptied Himself by assuming the form of a slave taking on the likeness of men. And when He had come as a man in his external form...." Jesus is equal with God but the head of the relationship is God the Father. This passage from 1 Corinthians is not about rights; it is about roles. It is about playing the proper role. In 1 Corinthians 10:4-5, Paul entered into a discussion about proper attire when one is praying. The Jewish custom of attire was that a woman would pray with her head covered and a man would pray without his head uncovered. To rebel against one's proper role was dishonoring to one's head. Ultimately it dishonored God. This would be the equivalent of saying, "I don't believe that God is really in control of everything." Therefore, the first principle when it came to dressing like one had some sense was to dress in a way that did not reject one's role in Christ.

Paul also had observed the Corinthians' **disgraceful attire**. He wrote in 1 Corinthians 10:6, "So if a woman's head is not covered, her hair should be cut off. But if it is disgraceful for a woman to have her hair cut off or her head shaved, she should be covered." To this day, Hebrew women wear what is called the *yashmak*. The *yashmak* is a veil covering the head and flowing all the way down to the feet. Remember that Corinth was noted as a city filled with immorality. It was a place notorious for prostitution; prostitutes did not wear these veils nor did they cut their hair. The Bible says the only reasons for a woman not to wear her veil would be that she had cut her hair in order to take a Nasserite vow, or she had shaved her head in mourning over the death of a family member. A prostitute would neither wear the veil nor would she cut her hair, thus revealing herself as a prostitute.

Different cultures have different taboos. I had the opportunity years ago to go on a short-term mission trip to Zambia in Africa. It was over one hundred degrees every single day that we were guests in that beautiful land. It was the middle of the summer. Our team prepared to go out to do some street witnessing on one of those one hundred degree days. That day I dressed in a pair of shorts and a T-shirt. I felt certain this would be appropriate for the heat of the day. The local pastor who was serving as my interpreter explained to me, "To show your knees in public in Zambia is considered to be lewd and vulgar." So what did I do? I could have argued, "This is the attire that I would dress in if I were in the States. I think this is acceptable." I could go against the culture, but in choosing to do so I would offend the very people I was trying to reach. I went back to my motel room, found a long pair of pants and proceeded with the day. That was a choice well made.

I heard a news story in 2007. Maybe you also saw the story of Kyla Ebbert. On Labor Day weekend that year, Kyla boarded a Southwest Airlines flight headed to Tucson, Arizona. The temperature in Tucson that day was 106 degrees in the desert. Two Southwest Airlines personnel escorted Kyla off the flight after numerous complaints that she was not dressed appropriately. She was allowed back on the plane only after she agreed to cover herself up with a provided blanket. When Kyla left the plane, a media circus formed in covering the event. She became a guest on almost every talk show; newspapers wrote editorials about her experience; bloggers began to make comments. I found one blogger who had quizzed Southwest Airlines as to whether someone could legally board their airplanes wearing a bikini. After the media hype, the question became whether this young lady misunderstood or did she just not know what was appropriate? Well, did this event change her life? Kyla took her fifteen minutes of fame, signed a contract with *Playboy* and literally revealed what her intentions were from the beginning.

There's an ancient document from the second century called the *Epistle to Diogenes*. A believer wrote the letter to a pagan, Diogenes, in an attempt to prove to him that the early movement known as Christianity was not merely passing fad. The letter states,

The Christians are not distinguished from other men by country or by language nor by civil institutions. For they neither dwell in cities by themselves nor use peculiar tongues; no lead a singular mode of life; they dwell in Grecian or Barbarian cities as the case may be. They follow the usage of their country in dress, food, and other affairs of life. Yet they present a wonderful and confessedly paradoxical conduct. They dwell in their own native lands but they do so as strangers.[3]

Principle number two is that our clothing should not bring reproach. The Christian's attire should be typical of what is normal and culturally acceptable.

The actions of the Corinthians indicated their **defiant attitudes**. 1 Corinthians 10:13-16 states,

> Judge for yourselves. Is it proper for a woman to pray to God with her head uncovered? Does not even nature itself teach you that if a man has long hair it is a disgrace to him? But then if a woman has long hair it is her glory? For her hair is given to her as a covering. But if anyone wants to argue about this, we have no other custom nor do the churches of God.

Paul had observed people trying to defy nature when it came to their dress. For some people their only reasoning behind what they did was an attempt to start an argument. Perhaps you have heard exasperated people claim, "Well, Jesus had long hair; I'm just trying to be an individual; I'm just trying to reveal my inner self." Principle number three when it comes to dress is that attire should not reflect a rebellious attitude. Dress should not indicate rebellion against authority: "I'm in rebellion against my parents; I'm in rebellion against the rules in my office; I'm in rebellion against cultural norms." Dress like you have some sense.

The Example of Interaction

Paul gave not only an example of intervention, to dress like one had some sense, but also an **example of interaction**. Paul pointed out that Christians needed to dine like they had some sense. Since the beginning of the church, it had been customary for Christians to enjoy eating together. Even today, this is not just a Baptist thing, it is a believer thing; people love to meet and eat. Acts 2:46-47 says, "Every day they devoted themselves to meeting together in the temple complex and broke bread from house to house. They ate their food with gladness and simplicity of heart." In the first century, the people of the church at Corinth loved to meet and eat. The early Corinthian church had developed a tradition known as the "love feast." This "love feast" was the ancient forerunner of the potluck supper. It was a shared meal observed every time the church partook of the Lord's Supper. They would pool their food and then share this great love feast. It was intended to be a time of tremendous fellowship.

Three problems had developed as a result of the love feast. First, there was a **segregation problem**. 1 Corinthians 10:17-18 indicates divisions had developed within the church. As mentioned earlier the word "divisions" translates the Greek word *schismata*, from which we get our English word *schisms*. The Corinthian Christians were obviously segregating themselves into little groups. Many Americans feel this country has overcome centuries of segregation. We have recently elected our first African-American president; this fact causes some to think segregation is no longer a problem in our society. However, after twenty-one centuries, segregation has continued in the church. This kind of segregation is not limited to racial bigotry. Think about your experiences at church. We sit with the people we know and often times in the same place every week. We tend to eat with the people we like, we enjoy fellowship with four to six families and we know very few people outside of this realm of fellowship. Then we wonder why someone from outside the church would claim the church is cliquish. There truly is a segregation problem in the church.

The church has not only a segregation problem, but also a **sharing problem**. 1 Corinthians 11:20-21 states, "Therefore, when you come together in one place it is not really to eat the Lord's Supper. For in eating each one takes his own supper ahead of others and one person is hungry while another is drunk!" The love feast had turned into a vanity buffet. Wealthy people were bringing food and not sharing it with the poor people of the congregation. The biblical record indicates that this abuse extended to some getting drunk before the Lord's Supper, as 1 John 3:17 says, "If anyone has this world's good and sees his brother in need but shuts off his compassion from him, how can God's love reside in him?" Similarly, in our day, 40,000 people die daily of hunger in this world, while Americans spend three billion dollars a year on pet food.[4] There is definitely a sharing problem in this world.

Economist Robert Heilbroner described what the average American would have to surrender to live like one of the one billion hungry people in the Third World. Here is what you and I would have to give up. Start with your home. You would have to strip it of all its furniture. Get rid of all the couches and all of the end tables. You could keep one kitchen table and one wooden chair—not a set, but *one* wooden chair. Move to your closet and you would have to get rid of all your clothes. Some of us need to clean out our closets anyway! You could keep your oldest suit or your oldest dress and your oldest shirt or your oldest blouse. One! Then you would move to the kitchen. This is an easy one. Every appliance, anything that plugs in, anything that makes your life easier—get rid of it! You could keep a box of matches. Move on to your cupboards filled with processed foods. Get rid of all that. Get rid of every processed food in your house, but you can keep a potato or two for your supper tonight, maybe a half-rotten onion. That would be the limit of your food supply, not only for today, but also for the next three days.

Thinking outside your home and you would need to get rid of every government service provided. There would be no police, no firefighters, and no one to deliver the mail. There might be a school three to five miles away; it would be a two-room schoolhouse at best. There would be no hospital, but there might be a free clinic at least ten miles away with the only means of transportation being a village bicycle. This would not be *your* bicycle, but one village bicycle that would be used by everyone in the entire community.

When it comes to money, you would have to get rid of all your credit cards and empty all your bank accounts. Pocket money lying around the house would need to be discarded. What you could keep would be the equivalent of less than five dollars in change. This past year an Iranian peasant died due to lack of medical care because he did not have $3.94 to see a physician. What he didn't know is that the physician would have seen him for free.[5] The average person in the church pew has no idea the enormity of the world's needs. And quite possible many prefer the comfortable position of their uninformed state.

The church has a segregation problem; the church has a sharing problem; and thirdly, the church also has a **superiority problem**. 1 Corinthians 11:22 says, "Don't you have houses to eat and drink in? Or do you look down on the church of God and embarrass those who have nothing? What should I say to you? Should I praise you? I do not praise you for this." If you are reading this book, it is highly probable that you are among the top one percent of the world's wealthiest individuals. How did we get to where we are today? How did you and I become one of the elite one percent of people in the world? You got here by God's choosing. God blessed you by your birth into an area and a family with a blessed opportunity. Few of us will experience even a fraction of the world's woes. As James 1:17 says, "Every generous act and every perfect gift is from above." So dress like you have some sense and dine like you have some sense.

The Example of Introspection

Paul's third example was an **example of introspection**. It leads us to make decisions as though we have some sense. Last chapter I shared with you about how to make godly decisions in the gray areas of life. Paul revisits this theme of how to make good decisions. 1 Corinthians 11:28 states, "So a man should examine himself; in this way he should eat of the bread and drink of the cup." We need regular evaluations in life. The military calls it an inspection. The dentist calls it a check up. A mechanic calls it a tune up. A teacher calls it a quiz.

An accountant calls it an audit. And the church calls it the Lord's Supper. It is a time of evaluation. It is a time of introspection.

When you partake of the Lord's Supper, look for four elements. First, there should be a **backward look**. 1 Corinthians 11:24-25 has a repeated theme, "Do this in remembrance of me." Paul told the Corinthians, "I want you to remember the record. I want you to remember how he died. I want you to remember why he died. I want you to recall every detail about the event." Romans 5:6 says,

> For while we were still helpless, at the appointed moment, Christ died for the ungodly. For rarely will someone die for a just person, though for a good person perhaps someone might even dare to die. But God proves his own love for us in that while we were still sinners, Christ died for us!

Look backward, remember the record; what Christ has paid for you.

The second look is an **inward look**. The question isn't whether or not we are sinners. The Bible declares that all of us are sinners. Romans 3:23 states, "All have sinned and fall short of the glory of God." The question is whether or not we have a relationship. Am I saved? Do I belong at the Lord's Table? Am I a member of the family? Philippians 1:6 says, "I am sure of this, that He who has started a good work in you will carry it to completion until the day of Christ Jesus." Look inwardly and review the reality of your relationship with Jesus Christ. Is God in charge of your life? Am you a member of his family?

The next look for Paul was a **forward look**. 1 Corinthians 11:26 says, "For as often as you eat this bread and drink the cup, you proclaim the Lord's death until he comes." We live in eager anticipation of the return of our Savior. 1 John 3:2 says, "We know that when He appears we will be like Him, because we will see Him as He is." One of the final cries of Scripture in the last chapter of the last book, says, " Even so, come, Lord Jesus" (Rev. 22:20). When I take a forward look, I need to be ready for Christ's return. So when I complete this evaluation, I have taken a backward look, remembering the record of what Christ has done for me. I have taken an inward look, reviewing the reality of whether I have a relationship with Christ. And I have taken a forward look, preparing for the Lord to return at any moment.

The final look Paul described was an **outward look.** The King James Version reads, "You show forth the Lord's death" (1 Cor. 11:26). The Greek word translated as "proclaim" or "show forth" was used in the first century to describe how a herald would come into the city and announce news. News! News! In his ministry, Paul commissioned heralds at every opportunity to announce the news of what Christ had done in their lives. Today, when I reflect upon the redemption of Christ changing me, I cannot keep that to myself.

William D. Hendricks, in his book, *Exit Interviews: Revealing Stories of Why People Are Leaving Church*, interviewed people who once were very actively involved and invested in the life of a church but have subsequently dropped out. Why were people leaving churches? Surprisingly the most common complaint was not the music, it wasn't the facility, and it wasn't the preaching. The most common reason people gave for leaving churches is that the church did not provide them with an opportunity to meet God. Hendricks wrote, "Apparently it doesn't matter if the service is entertaining. When interaction with God is absent, eventually the church will loose its appeal."[6] The Lord's Supper reminds us of the presence of God: "Do this in remembrance of me." He desires to have a relationship with us through his Son, Jesus Christ.

In a church where I had served as the pastor, a cantankerous lady came to every business meeting. I am talking about the kind of person who wanted to know the agenda of the business meeting and said, "What are we voting on today so that I know what I'm against." We had quarterly business meetings in this church. We also had quarterly observance of the Lord's Supper at this church. (By the way, there is no biblical mandate concerning how often you take the Lord's Supper. 1 Corinthians 11:25 says, "As often as you do this, do this in remembrance of me.") Our ministry staff determined that if we were going to have a quarterly business meeting and a quarterly observance of the Lord's Supper, why would we not put these two together? We would do the Lord's Supper on the same evening that we had our business conference. The cantankerous church lady approached me about our staff decision and said, "Pastor, I'm having problems taking the Lord's Supper and then going into the business meeting." I said, "Really? Could it be that you are actually having problems going into the business meeting after having taken the Lord's Supper?" She explained her position, saying, "The Lord's Supper just does not put me in the proper mood for a business meeting." I asked, "What would be the proper mood?" She started to hem, haw, stutter, and finally blurted out, "Well, I'm just filled with the love of Christ when I take the Lord's Supper." I quickly responded, "That is the proper mood you should have to go into a business meeting." Christians need to make decisions as though we have some sense of the presence of God every single day of our lives, because we do. "Do this as often as you do it, do it in remembrance of me" (1 Cor. 11.25).

The Lord's Supper should remind you of the presence of God in your life. If you need to do it daily, I would suggest you do it daily even if you had to do it by yourself. The Lord's Supper is to be a picture reminding you that God is in control and his presence in your life is real: "Do this as often as you do it, do it in remembrance of me" 1 Cor. 11:25) Act as if you have some sense of the presence of God in your life!

LESSON 9
PLAY TO YOUR
STRENGTHS

eter Drucker, the management expert, was quoted in *The Best of the Harvard Business Review, 1999,* "Only when you operate from a combination of your strengths and self-knowledge can you achieve true and lasting excellence."[1] When Drucker says something, the business world perks up its ears and immediately begins rushing to a conclusion. The result has been companies began to hire "strength coaches" to help employees learn their strengths and to optimize their impact upon the organization. Strength coaches could help one find what one is best at doing and how one can give one's best to the organization.

One such strength coach is a gentleman by the name of Marcus Buckingham. Marcus was the former leader of the Gallup Strength Management practice. Buckingham says,

> The best managers share one talent; the ability to find and then capitalize upon the employee's unique traits. The guiding principle is, how can I take this person's talent and turn it into performance. That is the only way success is possible. Bad managers play checkers, good managers play chess. The good manager knows that not all employees work the same. A great manager is brilliant at spotting the unique differences that separate each person and then capitalizing upon him or her. Bad managers play checkers, good managers play chess.[2]

In the game of checkers, all the pieces look alike. They all move in exactly same fashion; the strategy is so simple a child can understand it. Chess the pieces have different shapes. They have different capabilities of movement and the strategy becomes extremely complex. Bad managers treat everyone as if they are in a cookie-cutter world; everyone does things exactly the same way. Good managers realize that there are strengths to each person and that you use those strengths to optimize your pursuit of success.

The apostle Paul was a strength coach for the early church. He realized that God had given unique gifts to the church. Pastor John MacArthur says, "No local congregation will be what it should be; what Jesus prayed it would be; what the Holy Spirit and empowered it to be until it understands Spiritual gifts."[3] The New Testament gives much attention to the work of the Holy Spirit. The work of the Holy Spirit is mentioned in all but three books of the New Testament (Philemon and 2 and 3 John are the exceptions). Paul was the most prolific of writers in telling about the work of the Holy Spirit. He mentioned the Holy Spirit 120 times in his writings. And 1 Corinthians 12,14 are, for us, his survey course on the gifts of God's Spirit.

Remember that in the beginning of his writing, in 1 Corinthians 1:7, Paul indicated that Corinth was outstanding in its gifts of the Spirit. He said, "You do not lack any spiritual gift." Paul realized that the Holy Spirit was not merely a doctrine in which to believe; the Holy Spirit was a person to experience. Once one has experienced God's Spirit, then one will know how to perform the ministry one has received from God.

Recall the Corinthians were noted for their division in the church. Spiritual gifts just provided them with another opportunity to divide. Rick Warren, in *The Purpose Driven Life*, says there are two main problems when one begins to think about spiritual gifts. One is gift envy. That happens when one think that one's own spiritual gift isn't equal to or isn't quite the same as someone else's gift. This leads one to feel envy for someone else's Spiritual gift. The other problem is gift projection. This is the idea my spiritual giftedness should dictate the way everyone perceives or perform. I expect everyone to do things exactly the way that I do them. These same two problems, gift envy and gift projection, have plagued the church for twenty-one centuries. Here is Paul's advice: realize that you are individually and personally gifted by the Spirit and optimize what you have to give for the purposes of God's kingdom.

The Source of Spiritual Gifts

Paul, the strength coach, gave us four principles for a clear understanding of the spiritual gifts through his writings to the Corinthians. The first principle is the **source of spiritual gifts**. In 1 Corinthians 6:20, Paul wrote, "Your body is a sanctuary of the Holy Spirit who is in you." At conversion you became the **dwelling place** of the Holy Spirit. The Holy Spirit took up permanent residence inside of you, not as a temporary guest, not by taking a guest room. but by making you a dwelling place of the Holy Spirit. We do not need to sing, "Come, Holy Spirit." If you are a believer in the Lord Jesus Christ, Jesus' Spirit lives within you!

In 1 Corinthians 12:3, Paul wrote, "Therefore, I am informing you that no one speaking by the Spirit of God says 'Jesus is cursed,' and no one can say, 'Jesus is Lord,' except by the Holy Spirit." How does one reconcile that verse with Jesus' teaching in the Sermon on the Mount, where he said, "Not everyone who says to me 'Lord, Lord,' shall enter the Kingdom of Heaven" (Matt. 7:21)? The key to the Corinthian text is the word "cursed." In the first century persecutors of the church attempted to get the early Christians to renounce their faith and to declare, "Caesar is Lord." A historian by the name of Trajan told about a governor named Pliny who burned Christians at the stake. Polycarp, the Bishop of Smyrna, was told to renounce his faith and to worship Caesar or die. Polycarp responded, "Eighty and six years I have served Christ and He has never done me wrong. How can I blaspheme my King who saved me"? Later Historians tell us that when Polycarp was burned at the stake, he requested that his ropes be loosed after he was set on fire so that he could clap his burning hands together while singing with his dying breath, "None But Jesus, Jesus Only." The Holy Spirit certainly dwelt in Bishop Polycarp. When the Holy Spirit genuinely dwells inside a believer, the Spirit can stand the heat. When others are telling you to give up your faith, to give up Jesus Christ, and to renounce who you are in him, the Holy Spirit will stand the heat for you as well.

The second aspect of the source of gifts is the **distribution by the Spirit**. In 1 Corinthians 12:4-6, there appears a constant and a variable. The constant is always the same. The variable is always changing, always different. In 1 Corinthians 12:4, the text says there are "different gifts." The word *gift* is the translation of *charismata*. This is where we get our word *charismatic*. It is a compound word in Greek, with *charis* meaning grace and *mata* meaning gift. Grace gifts. There are different gifts given to us by the grace of God. According to the verse, however, there is one Spirit—different gifts, but the same Spirit. The next verse tells that there are "different ministries." The Greek word is *diakonai*, from which we derive our English word *deacon*, meaning servant. "There are different ways of serving but there is only one Lord" (1 Cor. 12:5).

1 Corinthians 12:6 states that there are "different activities." The word "activities" is the translation of the Greek *energemata*. We get the English word *energy* from this root. There are different ways of doing things—different energies—but there is one God. The constant is God and the variable is how he expresses himself through believers. Then the next verse says a manifestation of the Spirit is given to each person to produce something beneficial. God works through each of us individually and personally. Take, for example, the gift of preaching or prophesying. The ministry could be manifest in someone becoming a pastor, evangelist, missionary, or a teacher; the activity could be that some shout, some sit on a stool, and some teach by making all the points start with the same letter.

God is the constant, while the variable is how he works through individuals and their personalities. 1 Corinthians 12:11 says, "But one in the same Spirit is active and all these distributed unto each one as He wills." The emphasis is "as *He* wills." Every believer has a gift. However, no one believer has all the gifts.

When I first began in ministry, a movement, known as the "Full Gospel" movement, swept across America. "Full Gospel" meant believing in all the gifts. This often was interpreted to mean that anyone could obtain all the spiritual gifts by merely petitioning God for them. A staff member in a church I had served underwent a spiritual gifts inventory (Spiritual gift inventories do not determine one's spiritual gifts but rather the propensity one has for certain gifts). When he scored his test he had all the spiritual gifts. That was the way this young man perceived himself, as possessing all of the gifts. Every believer has a gift. No believer has all the gifts. God is the distributor of the gifts. God gives them as he wills. He is the source of spiritual gifts.

The Service of Spiritual Gifts

The second principle Paul spelled out to aid in understanding spiritual gifts was the **service of spiritual gifts**. This includes not only the gifts' origins, but also how one uses them. How does one put them into practice in the church or in one's life? When one puts gifts into practice, a **coordinated effort** is needed. The Bible describes believers with several pictorial phrases; one of them describes the believer as a part of a body. This was one of Paul's favorite metaphors. He used it ninety-one times in his writing. To be a member of the body and then to be separate or segregated from the body would be disgusting. I love beautiful eyes, but I don't love them separated from the body. That is just disgusting and gross. Further, if a body part is separated from the body long enough, then that body part dies.

Hebrews 10:25 says, "Not forsaking the assembling of ourselves together as is the manner of some is but exhorting one another, and so much the more as you see the Day approaching" (NKJV). Paul again used some of his sacred sarcasm. 1 Corinthians 12:15-16, Paul pictured body parts having arguments with one another. A body part with an inferiority complex says, "I am not important; I'm not as useful as that other body part." I hear that conversation in the hallways at church on any given Sunday. "No one notices when I'm not here, I'm just not as important." Paul asked in 1 Corinthians 12:17, "What if we were all alike? What if the body was just one big eyeball? What if we were all exactly the same thing?" Not only would that be boring, it would also indeed be disgusting. Imagine a church full of people who are exactly like you! In 1 Corinthians 12:18-20, Paul explained that God put us together. But then God placed the parts, each one of them in the body, just as he wanted. If they were all the same part, where would the body be? Now there are many parts and yet one body. God put us together. He coordinated this effort.

Gifts work in service together as a **collaborative effort**. In 1 Corinthians 12:21-22, Paul pointed out that not only did God put people together in a coordinated fashion, but he also did so because they needed one another. The eye cannot say to the hand, "I don't need you," nor again the head to the feet, "I don't need you." On the contrary, those parts of the body that appear to be weaker are necessary. As parts of the body, we need one another. We are mutually dependent upon one another. It is being a member of a marching band, where all of the members play different instruments simultaneously in order to bring music to life. Believers are intertwined intentionally. God made us this way intentionally so we might work collaboratively in ministry.

1 Corinthians 12:26 embodies what I call my "big toe theology." The verse states, "So if one member suffers, all the members suffer with it; if one member is honored, all the members rejoice with it." I call this my big toe theology because I have noticed when you hit your big toe in the middle of the night, you don't just hurt in the big toe. You hurt all the way up to the top or your head. It sends chills all the way up your spine; your arms hurt; everything hurts. What you might consider to be a small and insignificant member of the body is hurting! So, when one member of the body suffers, we all suffer; we hurt with each other and we rejoice with one another. This is a coordinated and collaborative effort.

The Significance of Spiritual Gifts

Paul shared the third principle in understanding spiritual gifts, the **significance of spiritual gifts**. In 1 Corinthians 12:27-28, he wrote, "Now you are the body of Christ; [the service of spiritual gifts] and individual members of it. And God has placed these in the church [the source of spiritual gifts]." I have given these to you, God says, and I have done so for you to perform your ministry as a part of the body. Paul gave an **inventory of the church**, a listing of spiritual gifts. This is not a complete list. It is a sample list. There are other lists in the New Testament, including those in Ephesians 4 and Romans 12. Bible scholars have attempted to combine these lists. I have seen a compiled list of nineteen spiritual gifts, another list of twenty-six spiritual gifts, and yet another list of twelve spiritual gifts. Regardless of the number of gifts, Paul asked several rhetorical questions. "Are all apostles?" The answer to that was a "no." "Are all prophets?" No. "Are all teachers?" No. "Do all do miracles?" Does anyone have all of the gifts, and the answer is no.

A very cursory observation of the list of gifts in 1 Corinthians indicates there are some "limelight" gifts and some behind-the-scene gifts. 1 Corinthians 12:31 states, "Desire the greater gifts. And I will show you and even better way." This raises the question, "What are the greater gifts?" Which of the gifts of the Spirit are the greater ones? After an interlude where Paul talked about the proper attitude in exercising spiritual gifts in 1 Corinthians 13, (the great Love Chapter), he gave an answer in 1 Corinthians 14 about how one measures the greatness of spiritual gifts.

Paul's first measure of greatness was the **importance of comprehension**:

> Pursue love and desire spiritual gifts and above all that you may prophesy. For the person who speaks in another language is not speaking to men but to God, since no one understands him; however, he speaks mysteries in the Spirit. But the person who prophesies speaks to people for edification, encouragement and consolation (1 Cor. 14:1-3).

A key word in making sense of 1 Corinthians 14 is the word "understanding." The word "understand" appears five times in just the first nineteen verses. We're reminded that we cannot perform a task unless we understand the instructions. Paul gave three illustrations where understanding is key. In 1 Corinthians 14:7, he gave the illustration of an **unclear chime**. Paul explained that even inanimate things, like a flute or harp, produce sounds. If they don't make distinctive notes, how will the flute or harp be recognized? Have you ever heard an instrument that is really out of tune? I'm talking about the sound that makes everyone's head turn just a little bit, their eyes begin to squint, and then the dogs in the neighborhood begin to bark. An instrument out of tune is of no value to the orchestra or band; it is an unclear chime.

The second illustration Paul gave was an **unclear call**: "In fact if the trumpet makes an unclear sound, who will prepare for the battle (1 Cor. 14:8)?" That takes me back to my days as a Boy Scout. I never served in the military, but I was in the Boy Scouts and we did have a Boy Scout bugler. Our troop's bugler was a trumpeter beginning to learn to play the bugle. He had one primary problem. He could only sound one note. If you can only sound one note on the bugle, then "charge" cannot be distinguished from the call for retreat. That is not a serious difficulty when it comes to the Boy Scouts, but it is critical when it comes to the military.

Paul's third illustration was an **unclear conversation**. 1 Corinthians 14:11 states, "Therefore, if I do not know the meaning of the language, I will be a foreigner to the speaker and the speaker will be a foreigner to me." My wife, Glenda, had an experience in Atlanta's airport. Atlanta has one of the largest airports in the world. A good number of international flights pass through its terminal. Glenda observed a gentleman who appeared to be of Asian descent with few English skills struggling to be able to communicate. This man would point to his ticket and then gesture to Glenda, asking if this train would take him to his gate. Glenda nodded her head yes; then the Asian gentleman boarded the train. The train made frequent stops at every set of gates, so it stopped at the first set of gates. The gentleman started to get off the train. Glenda waved her arms, exclaiming, "No, no, not here, not here!" The train stopped at the second set of gates and Glenda gave what she thought to be the international symbol for "get off the train," moving one arm in a welcoming directional motion towards the exit. He didn't get it. Glenda then pushed him towards the exit. The man pointed at his ticket once again. Glenda nodded a "yes" and he finally got off the train. We encounter difficulties when language is a barrier. God wants us to teach people so that they understand. God wants us to be able to communicate so that others can "get it." God has given each of us a spiritual gift with the primary purpose of aiding others in understanding who he is.

My first published work is *Discover the Witness Inside of You*. It is a guide for how to use your spiritual gift to share your faith. Many people say, "I don't have the spiritual gift of evangelism," or "Because I have the spiritual gift of mercy or helps, then I have an excuse for not fulfilling the Great Commission." The Great Commission was given to all people, regardless of their spiritual gifts. God intended for you to discover your spiritual gift and to use it to communicate the gospel of Jesus Christ.

Recently I read this posting on a pastor's blog:

> Too many Christians are not serving. When you ask them to do something they say, well, sorry but that is not my spiritual gift. The trouble is they seem to think that they don't have any spiritual gift because they say that about everything I ask them to do. Brethren, I tell you the truth in Christ that there are no such gifts as pew warming or sermon listening or music enjoying. All of the Spiritual gifts are proactive. You DO something. If you tell me that you are sold out to the Lord and you are not doing anything for Him, then you are being a liar. How do you explain the idea of being consecrated to the Lord or surrendered to the Lord if you are not willing to use what God gave you?

The Standards of Spiritual Gifts

Paul's final principle for understanding spiritual gifts was to know the **standards of spiritual gifts**. In the last couple of paragraphs of Chapter 14, Paul's summary begins. Remember that Paul was giving advice to a church in reply to questions about which they had written him. One of the Corinthians' problems was that they were divided over spiritual gifts. Can you imagine they were divided because they were so gifted in their church? 1 Corinthians 14:20 says, "Brothers don't be childish in your thinking, but be infants in evil and adult in your thinking." We learn from this that if we are going to be childish about something, be infantile in the way in which we look at evil, but be adult in the way in which we look at God. Paul outlined two standards to aid in one's understanding of spiritual gifts.

The first standard is **clarity of message**. Any sermon or teaching concerning spiritual gifts eventually gets around to the gift of speaking in tongues or unknown languages. This passage offers guidelines that I have not dealt with in detail. But 1 Corinthians 14:21 states, "It is written in the Law by people of other languages and by the lips of foreigners, I will speak to this people; and even then, they will not listen to me." If you desire to speak in another language as your spiritual gift, Paul said, then remember this Old Testament admonition from Isaiah 28:11-12. The people heard in their own language a warning from God and they refused to heed it. Because they heard the warning from God and refused to heed it, then they were taken into captivity in Assyria. In captivity they had the opportunity to hear a foreign language for a long, long time. Paul made clear that this was not the focus of spiritual gifts. Thus spiritual gifts are not about desiring something that one does not have. 1 Corinthians 14:22 explains that speaking in another language is intended as a sign, not to believers, but to unbelievers, while prophecy is not for unbelievers but for believers.

Conviction comes with understanding God's plan for one's life. Therefore, the most important question behind exercising spiritual gifts is, "Am I communicating the gospel; am I clarifying the message; am I helping someone else to see Jesus through what I am doing?"

Romans 10:14-18 states,

> How can they call on Him in whom they have not believed? And how can they believe without hearing about Him? And how can they hear without a preacher? And how can they preach unless they are sent? As it is written: How welcome are the feet of those who announce the gospel of good things! But all did not obey the gospel. For Isaiah says, Lord, who has believed our message? So faith comes from what is heard and what is heard comes through the message about Christ. But I ask, 'Did they not hear?' Yes, they did.

My first job after Glenda and I married was as a custodian in a nursing home. I worked there during the week and was the associate pastor of a small rural church on the weekends. I was thrust into a situation where most of my co-workers did not attend church. Many of them worked every weekend. But one young man about my age was turned off to church altogether. Eventually I found out why. I learned that as a youngster he had attended a church with his grandparents where things were not done "decently and in order." People in this church were speaking in an unknown language and this practice frightened the young man. I recalled a passage, and I read it for him. 1 Corinthians 14:23 says, "Therefore if the whole church assembles together, and all are speaking in other languages, and people who are uninformed or unbelievers come in, will they not say that you are out of your minds?" The entire purpose of the church coming together is not so people can see show off their spirituality. The purpose is to prepare us to share the goodness of God with the world.

Paul's second standard in evaluating spiritual gifts was the **construction of ministry**. 1 Corinthians 14:26 states, "How is it then brothers? Whenever you come together, each one has a psalm, a teaching, a revelation, another language, or an interpretation. All things must be done through edification." The chapter concludes, "But everything must be done decently and in order" (1 Cor. 14:40). Paul said the guiding principle for using spiritual gifts is to build up the faith. Paul instructed the church in how to accomplish this: "For you can all prophesy one by one, so that everyone may learn and everyone may be encouraged" (1 Cor. 14:31). The church is about edification and not about exhibition. This is what discipleship is all about. God has given us gifts; this is the source. He has done this so that we might work together in the body in a coordinated and collaborative effort; this is the service. The significance is so that we might be capable of sharing the message with a world that so desperately needs to hear that God has changed our lives. The guiding principles are clarity of message and construction of ministry.

Bertoldo de Giovanni is a name that even the most avid of art enthusiasts probably do not hear often. But he is significant because he was a student of Donatello, the greatest sculptor of his time. Giovanni was also the teacher of Michelangelo, probably the greatest sculptor of all time. Giovanni realized that people who are exceptionally gifted could become bored with everyday tasks and need to be challenged. So he pushed Michelangelo. Giovanni realized his gifts were so extraordinary that Michelangelo needed to be challenged daily. The story has it that Giovanni came into his art studio one day and Michelangelo was working on a sculpture that was beneath his skills, so beneath his gifts that Bertoldo went across the room, took a hammer and smashed the sculpture into a million pieces. He shouted to Michelangelo, "Talent is cheap but dedication is costly; dedicate yourself to your talent."[4]

Paul the strength coach challenged the Corinthians by saying, in essence, "Talent is cheap, and God gave it to you. You did nothing to earn these abilities God gave you. God gave it to you, but dedication is costly. Dedication is a willingness to give these talents back to God in his service. It is learning to play to your strengths!"[5]

LESSON 10
LEARN TO
LOVE 'EM

I am a huge fan of *The Andy Griffith Show*. I believe I have seen every episode at least a dozen times. My favorite episode of all time is episode number 43 (the fact that I know that it is episode number 43 indicates what kind of fan I am). The name of this episode is "Pickle Story." Those of us who are fans of the show know of it as "Kerosene Cucumbers." There is actually an Andy Griffith fan club called the "Kerosene Cucumbers," named after episode 43. For those not connoisseurs of *The Andy Griffith Show*, the storyline goes like this. Aunt Bee knows that everything homemade is better than that which is store-bought, so she makes a large batch of homemade pickles every year. The only problem is she makes horrible pickles. Andy has to find a way to get rid of them. He and Barney give the bad pickles to a passerby and then fill her empty pickle jars up with store bought pickles that they could actually eat. The store-bought pickles are so good that Aunt Bee decides to enter them into the County Fair contest. Knowing it would not be fair for Aunt Bee to win a rigged pickle contest, Andy and Barney eat up the good pickles, leading Aunt Bee to make another batch of pickles. She makes another batch of her kerosene cucumbers and enters them in the county fair.

The closing line of this show is one of the classic lines of all the Andy Griffith episodes. Her pickles obviously do not win, but now there is a whole new batch Andy and Barney are going to have to eat. Andy turns to Barney at the end of the county fair contest and says,

"We need to do what we should have done to begin with." Barney says, "What's that?" Andy says, "Learn to love 'em."

For some of you, the advice to love church people is about as palatable as trying to stomach one of Aunt Bee's kerosene cucumbers. Your face begins to shrivel up and your stomach begins to tie itself into knots. In the first chapter, I shared this quotation: "To live above with saints we love, oh that will be glory. But to live below with saints we know, oh now that's another story."[1] Jonathan Swift, the author of *Gulliver's Travels*, once said, "We have just enough religion to hate, but not enough to make us love." How prophetic that is of the church today.

1 Corinthians 13 is often referred to as the "Great Love Chapter." My preaching professor in seminary twenty-plus years ago was Doctor Luther Joe Thompson, the long-time pastor of the First Baptist Church, Richmond, Virginia. He wrote a book based on 1 Corinthians 13 entitled, *Love is Alive*. In that book, he states that love has no meaning until it becomes tangible.[2] In other words, love is not real until it is practiced and not merely preached. There is an old Irish proverb that says, "Money can buy a fine dog but only love will make him wag his tail." There are so many people who have not learned the lesson of love. Is love alive today? An even more important question is this: "Is love alive in the church today?"

1 Corinthians 13 is a favorite text of many people because they heard it read at their weddings. I have looked back over twenty-eight years of ministry and I have performed about one hundred weddings. I believe that 1 Corinthians 13 was read in ninety-five of them (including my three daughters' weddings). This chapter speaks about love, but marriage is not the context of the writing. Paul had been chastising the members of the church in Corinth for taking one another to court. He had chastised them for turning their heads to known sin within the body of Christ. He had chastised them for dividing over leadership issues in the life of the church. He had chastised them for being puffed up with pride about their own personal spiritual gifts. Then, in 1 Corinthians 13, he said, basically, "What you Corinthians need to learn is how to love one another. There is not a single problem that exists in the church that could not be dealt with by learning a good lesson on love."

Four different Greek words are all translated with the one English word, "love." Love is such a complex word in the English language. It is used for a variety of different emotions. For instance, the Greek word *eros* is the root of our word "erotic." It is the word for physical love. It is the natural attraction that takes place between a man and a woman. The second Greek word for love is *storge.* It is the word for family love. This is the word for how parents love their children, for parental love. The third Greek word is *phileo.* Philadelphia is referred to as the "city of brotherly love." This is the word for Platonic love. It is the love between friends. But none of these three words, *eros, storge, or phileo*, appears in 1 Corinthians 13. A fourth word for love is *agape.* This was actually a word created to communicate how believers ought to love one another. It is the word used to describe how God loves us in the giving of his Son, Jesus. If there were a definition for agape love, it would say, "Doing what is best for others without any regard for oneself." If *eros* is physical love and *storge* is parental love and *phileo* is Platonic love, *agape* is perfect love. This is the word used repeatedly in 1 Corinthians 13. God wants us to understand how to have this perfect love for one another. We need to learn how to love 'em.

Love Is an Essential

Paul wanted the early church to realize that love is the key. He opened this chapter by reminding us that **love is essential**. Paul declared that one can posses any spiritual gift, but without love, the gift is absolutely useless. For instance, Paul said in 1 Corinthians 13:1 that **praising without love is noise**. The fact that he began with the gift of languages indicated by all probability this was one of the most abused of the spiritual gifts. Heathen worship in the first century was characterized by the use of trumpets and cymbals and loud noises. Paul was equating worship services in which there was no love with satanic rituals. We need to be careful in this world of exclusivists who claim that they have "it" and therefore everyone needs to get "it," whatever "it" is. Praising God without loving the world is nothing more than noise to the ears of God. Praise without love is noise.

In 1 Corinthians 13:2, Paul said that **preaching without love is nothing**. You can divide preachers typically into two categories.

There are those who love souls. They love people and they love people so much that they want them to come to Christ. And then there are those who dangle hearers over an open pit opening into hell as if they are glad that they are headed there.

I was listening to a famous television evangelist preaching against abortion and he made a statement to the congregation that "all the legislatures who vote for this abortion law—they are all going to go to hell." When he completed that proclamation, the congregation erupted into applause. I pondered, are they applauding because people are going to hell? The Bible says in Ephesians 4:15, "Speak the truth in love." I thought of some of the great pulpiteers like Jerry Vines, Adrian Rogers, and Jim Henry. Men, who upheld the truth, held it high, and spoke the truth in love. To paraphrase Paul, "You can preach like Billy Graham and not have love, and it would be absolutely worthless."

Later in 1 Corinthians 13:2, Paul wrote, "You can understand all mysteries and all knowledge." In other words, you can hold degrees from Bible institutions, you could have taught Sunday school for twenty years, you can be a great Bible student and a great Bible scholar, and yet, if you don't have love, it is all worthless. At the close of the verse Paul said one may have faith like the faith that would move mountains, but even that faith can become fickle without love.

During the great inquisitions, the inquisitors had faith, but they thought that it was necessary to torture—even to the point of death—people who did not believe exactly like they did. We have our own brand of torture today. It may not be torture unto death, but we call it the cold shoulder of Christian fellowship. If others do not believe as I do or accept the same tenets that I accept, then I cannot share fellowship with them. Preaching without love is nothing.

Paul also instructed his readers that **philanthropy without love is nominalized**. There is nothing more humiliating than charity that takes place without love attached. Some people give to charity only because it eases their conscience or to inflate their egos. Paul even accused some of the early martyrs of having done this. In a church I had served, we went through a building program. I was asked by our building committee to recognize publicly the people in our congregation who had given a certain dollar amount or more. I refused, and the reason is not because I did not believe in recognizing people for extraordinary sacrifice. However, someone who has given less than the threshold amount may have made a much greater sacrifice than someone who had given the set amount or greater. The language in Paul's text implies that it is possible to act philanthropically without the motive of love underlying the action.

So one may preach like Billy Graham, sing like an award-winning artist, teach Sunday School for 20 years, give half of one's income to the church, and have ten Bible diplomas hanging on the wall, but if one does not have love, it is all absolutely worthless. Here is a biblical equation, "Everything, minus love, equals nothing." No matter what it is, if love is not involved, it is useless to God for the kingdom's purposes.

Let me give you a brief biblical love summary. The Bible teaches that Christians are to love one another. 1 Thessalonians 4:9 states, "You yourselves are taught by God, love one another." God taught us how to love one another by sending his Son. I John 4:19 states, "We love because He first loved us." Christ taught us that the greatest attribute of love is sacrifice. Then John 13:34-35 states, "I give you a new commandment: love one another. Just as I have loved you, you must also love one another. By this, all people will know that you are My disciples, if you have love for one another." The Bible states that when one becomes a believer, the Holy Spirit comes to dwell within and the Holy Spirit pours love into one's heart. Paul wrote in Romans 5:5, "God's love has been poured into our hearts through the Holy Spirit." Therefore, love must be essential.

Love Is Effectual

Love is not only essential, but **love is also effectual**. Love works! In 1 Corinthians 13:4-7, a paragraph describes what love looks like when it goes to work, when it is exhibited, when it is portrayed in a believer's life. Such love has three characteristics. The first is that love is **kindly patient**. This is one of the basic attributes of parental love, to be patient and kind. Your fondest memory of childhood may be when someone loved you when you didn't deserve to be loved, when someone loved you in spite of yourself, when someone displayed patient kindness towards you. I think of the example in the New

Testament of Jesus dealing with a woman caught in adultery. Jesus said to the woman, "Go and sin like this no longer" (John 8:11). I read a story this past week of a couple that had lost their son in World War II and they prayed for five minutes that they could be with their son again alive. Five minutes! An angel came down from heaven to answer their prayer and said, "What five minutes of your son's life would you like to revisit? Would you want the five minutes where you first held him in your arms and you dedicated him to God? Would you like the five minutes of the first day that you sent him off to school and you knew he was growing up? Would you like five minutes of one of your family vacations where it seemed like your family would never be separated? Would you like the five minutes on the day that you sent him off into the military? Or would you like the last five minutes with him on the battlefield?" The parents responded to the angel and said, "We want the day in which he came to us with his head bowed low because he had been playing in the garden, uprooted some plants, and before he could even speak, we said, 'We forgive you and we love you.'" Love is kindly patient.

James 1:4 in the King James Version states, "Let patience have her perfect work that ye may be perfect and entire and wanting nothing." Patience is the key to every perfect work. The Living Bible translates 1 Corinthians 13:4-5 to say, "never jealous or envious, never boastful or proud, never haughty or selfish or rude. Love does not demand its own way. It is not irritable or touchy. It does not hold grudges and will hardly even notice when others do it wrong." In the King James Version, 1 Corinthians 13:5 reads, "Love thinketh no evil." The Holman Christian Standard version translates that verse as saying, "It does not keep a record of wrongs." The word "thinketh" means to write down into a ledger. Love is not a scorekeeper. Love is not always keeping track of every time that something has gone wrong in a relationship.

Peter needed to learn the lesson of love. In Matthew 18:21, Peter came to Jesus and said, "Lord, how many times could my brother sin against me and I forgive him? As many as seven times?" Peter was extremely proud of his answer because he knew it was way beyond what the Pharisees were teaching. But Jesus responded, "I tell you not as many as seven…but seventy times seven." You cannot begin to count the number of times that you need to forgive. Love is not blind; it is not that love sees nothing wrong in the world. Love has a kindly patient, forgiving spirit.

Love at work is also characterized by being **knowingly pure.** Have you ever noticed children revel in wrongdoing? It is a mark of immaturity. One five-year-old child at a church where I had served would run and kick adults in the shins every Sunday. His mom would say, "Isn't that cute?" I said, "Let him kick *you* in the shins and see if you still think it is cute." It might have been somewhat cute when he was eighteen months to two years old. Can you imagine a twenty-year-old coming up and kicking you in the shins? There eventually needs to be growth in maturity. In 1 Corinthians 13:6, Paul pointed to those who take pleasure in unrighteousness, which is a mark of immaturity. Now it is time to grow up! Knowing what to do is not the problem the church faces. Everybody seems to know the right thing to do, the question becomes, "why don't we just do it?"

Love is knowingly pure, it recognizes that God has a plan and a purpose for one's life. When I love this way, I know the right thing to do and I am excited about the truth. I get excited about what God wants. I move beyond rejoicing in unrighteousness and I begin to rejoice in the truth.

Paul then sketched out the third characteristic love was **keenly perseverant**. 1 Corinthians 13:7 says, "Love bears all things, believes all things, hopes all things and endures all things." Energy is the force that moves an object. It is the wind that moves the windmill. Energy is the electricity that flows through a circuit. The Energizer Bunny commercials remind us that he can just "keep going and going and going." Love is the energy behind the Christian life. Love will stand when all else fails. Love bears the bad. Love empowers us to believe in one another. Love hopes for a better day and another opportunity. And love endures until the Lord returns. Love is kindly patient. Love is knowingly pure, and love is keenly perseverant. Paul has depicted how love is essential. Everything minus love is nothing. Love is also effectual; it works. I have seen it work in people's lives.

Love Is Eternal

Paul also taught his readers that **love is eternal**. In 1 Corinthians 13:8-10, he explained the **permanence of love**. Paul said, "Love never ends." Three gifts serve as signs, according to the list Paul shared: the gift of prophecy, the gift of languages or tongues, and the gift of the word of knowledge. Paul explained that these gifts are all temporary, but love is permanent. Song of Solomon 8:7 says, "Mighty waters cannot extinguish love; rivers cannot sweep it away." 1 Corinthians 13:10 states that "when that which is perfect has come" all these other things will have passed away. When do these gifts cease? "When that which is perfect has come." There are two basic interpretations to this phrase. Some scholars have said it occurred when the Scriptures were canonized. When the Scriptures became complete, when the sixty-six books were canonized, was when "that which is perfect has come." A second interpretation looked to the return of Christ. When Jesus returns to rapture the church, then "that which is perfect is come." Numerous fights over these two theories have taken place in doctrinal circles. I have a strong suspicion that this debate misses the key teaching of the passage: the gifts are temporary. They are only for here and now. Love is eternal. Which is more important? Trying to debate when the gifts will be done away with or trying to understand "what love's got to do with it?"

The second aspect of the eternal nature of love is the **perfection of love**. Two analogies appear in 1 Corinthians 13:11-12. Paul said, "When I was a child, I spoke like a child, I thought like a child, I reasoned like a child. When I became a man, I put away childish things." When we grow up, we don't need to act like children anymore. A child says, "I have to have it my way." A child thinks, "I am the most important person in this world." A child argues, "You need to agree with me." Paul warns that the childish way of looking at life needs to be set aside.

The second illustration Paul gives is that of looking into a mirror. He wrote, "Now we look in a mirror darkly or dimly." Mirrors in the first century were not made out of glass; they were made out of polished metal. The images were distorted and depended upon how old the metal was and how well it was polished. Using such mirrors, we would not see things very clearly. But one day, we will see him.

One day we will behold him. One day we will see him face to face. 1 John 3:2 says, "We know that when He appears, we will be like Him, because we will see Him as He is." The perfection of love is to finally see Jesus and see him just the way he is.

The final aspect of love's eternal nature is the **preeminence of love**. "And so faith, hope and love abide; these three, but the greatest of these is love." Faith without love is cold. Hope without love is grim. A famous pediatric doctor examined an abandoned child and said, "What this child needs more than anything else is love." What the world really needs is love. The world needs the love that is the essential kind of love; no spiritual gift can function without it. The world needs the kind of love that is the effectual; it is kindly patient and keenly perseverant and knowingly pure. The world needs the kind of love that is eternal love. When all the other gifts have passed away love will still remain.

When we think about love we often think about Valentine's Day as the holiday that celebrates love. This past Valentine's Day was one of the most special in my life. My precious wife, Glenda, expressed her love in a way that I will never forget. For the fourteen days leading up to Valentine's Day, she took one phrase of 1 Corinthians 13 and wrote me a love letter based upon the phrase, then left the love letter and a small gift on my desk for me to find every morning.

Valentine's Day is often the celebration of relational love for one another. Do you know where Valentine's Day actually originated as the holiday? Do you know the legend of St. Valentine? In the third century there was an oppressive ruler by the name of Claudius II. Claudius dared his subjects to worship the twelve gods whom he worshipped. He made it a crime, punishable by death to even affiliate with Christians. Valentinus was a devout Christian and was threatened with execution for the practice of his faith. He was arrested and imprisoned. During the final weeks before his execution, a jailor asked Valentinus if he could bring his daughter by the name of Julia to be schooled by the prisoner. The jailor's daughter had never been to a school. Julia was a pretty young girl with a sharp mind but she had been born blind. Valentinus taught her Roman history, arithmetic, but he also taught her about God and his love. Julia told Valentinus, "I wish that you would pray for me and pray that one day I will be able to see your face." Valentinus prayed for her from his prison cell. Julia saw a light and began to scream, "I can see, I can see, I can see!" Julia saw the face of her mentor Valentinus. On the eve of his death, Valentinus sent a letter to Julia urging her to stay close to God. The God who healed her would be the God that would direct her through the rest of her life. He signed it, "From your Valentine." The next day, February 14, 270, Valentinus was executed for his faith in the Lord Jesus Christ.[3]

Agape love is doing what is best for others without any regard for oneself. Romans 5:8 states, "God proves (or demonstrates) His own love for us in that while we were still sinners, Christ died for us." In John 15:13, Jesus said, "No one has greater love than this, that someone who would lay down his life for his friends." Two thousand years ago, our valentine sent us a love letter and said, "I'm willing to give my life for you, I want you to live your life for me."

LESSON 11
YOU MUST
BELIEVE!

am very fearful of this lesson sounding over-simplified and infantile. I want to be very careful to avoid that. I can remember as a child attending a stage presentation of the play *Peter Pan*. If you have seen *Peter Pan* in film or on stage you know that three-quarters of the way through the production Tinkerbelle the fairy dies. Peter Pan moves to the front of the stage and challenges the audience, "If you just believe, if everyone believes then Tinkerbelle can come back to life. If you believe, clap your hands." The audience erupts with applause and Tinkerbelle comes back to life. I do not think Paul addressed the Corinthians, saying that if they just believed to clap their hands. Believing is not something infantile or overly simple. Paul told the Corinthians that what one believes really does matter, because belief does affect our behavior.

My wife and I serve as hosts of a weekly Bible study group in our home. Recently we studied a video-based curriculum called *The Truth Project*. Focus on the Family Ministries produced this material. There is a dire need for us in the church to develop a Christian worldview and to be capable of explaining to the world why we believe what we believe. The very first lesson of *The Truth Project* challenges listeners with the question, "Do you really believe that what you really believe is really real?"[1] What one believes does affect behavior. Hebrews 11:6 says, "Without faith it is impossible to please God, for the one who draws near to Him must believe that He exists and He rewards those who seek Him." Belief is vital.

The Indianapolis Star reported in its March 9, 2008, edition the results of an Associated Press poll of Americans and religious life. The poll asked respondents to indicate their religious preference. Fifteen percent responded, "none or no religion."[2] This number has nearly doubled since the poll was taken in 1990 when it was 8.2 percent. Some skeptics of this data may say, "But that was a nationwide poll including those liberal West Coast people and the unchurched people of the Northeast. This does not reflect the Bible belt and it certainly is not accurate of my home area in the conservative Midwest." The next day, in the March 10 newspaper, a much smaller article broke down the same data to reflect just Indiana. The results to the same question in the Hoosier state were, "None— no stated religious preference, atheist or agnostic in Indiana— 8 percent in 1990, 15 percent in 2008," the exact same statistic that was in the nation wide survey.[3] Indiana is referred to as the "Crossroads of America" and a microcosm of everything America thinks. Once again this was proven to be true.

Dr. James Emory White. pastor, church consultant, and theologian has written a book entitled *Rethinking the Church*. In his book, White warns that our current culture is increasingly failing to believe. Dr. White writes, "72% of Americans deny the existence of absolute truth."[4] Why did Focus on the Family Ministry develop a Truth Project attempting to encourage the church to adopt and portray a Christian worldview? Because nearly three-quarters of Americans do not believe there is any such thing as absolute truth. Two out of three Americans do not know the very basic building block of our faith that "God so loved the world that He gave His only begotten Son" (John 3:16). We teach this to pre-school children in our Sunday School classes. Given the plight of our culture, no wonder less than four out of ten have any idea what the word "gospel" means. The word "gospel" means good news. We hear plenty of bad news every day. People need to know the good news of the gospel. Yet, there is an entire generation of biblically illiterate people (so much so that 10 percent believe that Noah's wife was Joan of Arc).[4] A generation may not know what to believe, but still we *must* believe!

You Must Believe the Scriptural Record

Paul told the Corinthians, "You must believe," but he also defined what must be believed. First of all one must believe in the **scriptural record**. Several years ago, a Newsweek poll declared that only one in three Americans believed that the Bible was the actual word of God and was therefore reliable. I am certain Paul·believed in the accuracy and reliability of Scripture. He believed it to be authoritative. In 1 Corinthians 15:3-4, both verses end "according to the scriptures." I memorized these verses years ago in a witness-training course. I always struggled remembering to put the "according to the scriptures" at the close of each verse. I wondered why the phrase was repeated. It was repeated not only for emphasis, but also for clarity. Paul said you must accept these things because they were scriptural accounts.

One might ask the question, "What scriptures?" The scriptures of the New Testament were being written at this time; the Scriptures that Paul was referring to were what we call the Old Testament. Paul told the Corinthians, right off the bat, if they wanted to know why they should believe, they should believe because of the scriptural accounts. This is a **converting word**. Remember, Paul was writing to relatively new believers. This was a new church and nearly everyone in this church had a recent and still-fresh experience of salvation. 1 Corinthians 15:1 says, "I proclaimed it, you received it and now you have taken your stand upon it." This should be the foundation of one's life, the teaching of these Scriptures. Psalm 19:7 in the New King James Version reads, "The law of the Lord is perfect, converting the soul and the testimony the Lord is sure, making wise the simple." In 1 Corinthians 15:2, Paul instructed them, saying this was the basis of their salvation, a converting word.

You must also believe in the scriptural account because it is a **cardinal word**. 1 Corinthians 15:3 states, "For I passed on to you as most important...." In this passage, Paul was saying, in effect, "The most important thing that I have to share with you is not advice about baptism, and is not about marriage and family life, and is not about the miracles of Jesus. The most important thing I have to share with you is the death, burial, and the resurrection of Jesus."

Romans 10:9-10 says, "If you confess with your mouth, 'Jesus is Lord,' and believe in your heart that God raised Him from the dead, you will be saved. With the heart one believes, resulting in righteousness, and with the mouth one confesses, resulting in salvation." According to this passage, belief in the resurrection is essential to salvation. When I was in seminary decades ago, the reality of Christ's resurrection was up for debate within scholarly circles. I actually had a seminary professor who stood up in a lecture one morning and claimed the resurrection was not real, that it was a spiritual metaphor. The professor taught in error that the resurrection of Jesus Christ has been the Spirit of Jesus resurrected in the life of the church. According to this misleading teacher, you and I are the resurrection of Jesus Christ. At the conclusion of this lecture, the professor asked, "Does that make me a liberal?" One very brave student raised his hand and said, "No, Professor, that makes you lost." Then the student read Romans 10:9-10 to the professor. The word resurrection means to "stand up." It is a physical term. It is a cardinal word; one must believe in the resurrection of Jesus Christ to be saved.

Paul maintained that one must also believe in the scriptural account because it was a **confirmed word**. Paul, while imprisoned in Rome, was witnessing to Festus. In Acts 26:26, Paul said, "For I'm not convinced that any of these things escapes the King's notice since this was not done in a corner!" The account of who Jesus is and the account of his resurrection is something that has been shared outside the circles of Christendom. There are historical records by both Christian and secular sources.

The scriptural records are difficult to deny, because **eyewitness accounts** appear in the Scriptures, with Paul enumerating five of them. He first mentioned that the risen Christ appeared to Peter, the same Peter who denied the Lord three times the night before his crucifixion. Then Paul said, "The Twelve" saw Jesus. This was a general term for the disciples; Thomas and Judas were absent but still the disciples would be referred to as "The Twelve." And then 500 brothers saw Jesus. This particular observance was only recorded here, but scholars believe this refers to the worship service cited in Matthew 28:16-17. In addition James, the half brother of Jesus Christ, who is not a believer until after the resurrection, saw the risen Lord. Then finally, Paul stated that the risen Christ was witnessed to "by other apostles." Literally, that would have included Thomas, the doubter. In total, Paul made reference to five recorded accounts of visible sightings of the resurrected Jesus. Jewish law required two witnesses to confirm an event.

Thus Paul presented overwhelming evidence. And if that were not enough, Paul said there were not only eyewitnesses to Jesus after his resurrection, but also **experiential witnesses** to Jesus. In 1 Corinthians 15:8, Paul explained, Jesus also appeared to him. Paul's experience was no less real than the experiences of the other apostles, just as your experience is just as real as theirs.

In the 1960s a disturbing movement infiltrated society, claiming, "God is dead." Dr. Billy Graham once told about the time an adopter of the "God is dead" philosophy approached him and asked, "Dr. Graham, don't you realize that God is dead?" The famous evangelist responded, "Really? I spoke with Him this morning." Our experiences are no less authentic than the New Testament's eyewitness accounts. Recall the words of Jesus who spoke to doubting Thomas in John 20:29, "Because you have seen me you have believed. Those who believe without seeing are truly blessed." One must believe in the scriptural record.

You Must Believe in the Savior's Resurrection

The second thing that Paul instructed the Corinthians they must believe in was the **Savior's resurrection**. Once a lady wrote to a newspaper advice column in her town, "Dear sirs, our preacher last Sunday said that Jesus just swooned on the cross; he faked it and the disciples nursed him back to health. What do you think? Sincerely, (signed) Bewildered." The newspaper's response followed, "Dear Bewildered, Beat your preacher with a cat of nine tails (a whip with metal in it), 39 times. Nail him to a cross, run a spear through his side, put him in an airless tomb for 36 hours and then see what happens to him."[5]

C.S. Lewis, one of the most noted Christian authors of recent generations, began his career as a devout atheist. Lewis set out to disprove the resurrection and declare Jesus officially dead. It was during his research that Lewis became convinced, convicted, and ultimately converted to the cause of Jesus Christ. Lewis learned that when one begins to examine the life of Christ and the accounts of the resurrection, one comes to one of three conclusions. First, Jesus is Lord and is who he claimed to be. He is the Son of God and the accounts of his miracles are correct. Second, Jesus was a liar and all who follow him are liars and are party to the lie. Third, Jesus was a stark-raving lunatic, making Christianity the greatest masquerade ever staged in the history of humanity.

Paul said, "What if there was no resurrection?" This passage states clearly the **priority of the resurrection**. In 1 Corinthians 15:12-19, Paul played the "What if?" game. Paul said that if there were not a resurrection, preaching would be fireless. Preaching would have no foundation without a resurrection. People would be faithless without a resurrection. The church would be declared fraudulent without a resurrection. 1 Corinthians 15:15 states, "We are found to be false witnesses." Death would be feared without a resurrection: "Those who have fallen asleep in Christ, they have also perished" (1 Cor. 15:18). Our life would be declared a failure without a resurrection, as 1 Corinthians 15:17 relates, "Your faith is worthless and you are still in your own sins." Our attitudes would be most forlorn without a resurrection: "If we have placed our hope in Christ for this life only, we should be pitied more than anyone" (1 Cor. 15:19). Paul placed the highest priority on the resurrection. He proclaimed that everything in life would fall apart without the resurrection.

Not only did he state the priority of the resurrection, but then in 1 Corinthians 15:20-23, Paul gave some **particulars of the resurrection**. "But now Christ has been raised from the dead, the first fruits of those who have fallen asleep" (1 Cor. 15:10). He described Christ's resurrection as the "first fruits." Leviticus 23 records that during the celebration of the Passover, the children of Israel were required to bring the first of their crop—the first of their yield—and lay it before the Lord as a symbol that the entire crop belonged to God. It was a symbol there was more to come.

When the Bible describes Jesus' resurrection as the first fruit, it implies Christ was the first to be resurrected from the dead. Christ's resurrection is the guarantee of our resurrection and a pattern which our resurrection will follow. In John 5:28-29, Jesus said, "Do not be amazed at this, because a time is coming when all who are in the graves will hear His voice and come out—those who have done good things, to the resurrection of life, but those who have done wicked things, to the resurrection of judgment."

Belief in the resurrection also involves the **product of the resurrection**. 1 Corinthians 15:24-26 says, "Then comes the end when He hands over the Kingdom of God the Father, when He abolishes all rule and all authority and power. For He must reign until He puts all His enemies under His feet. The last enemy to be abolished is death." This is the ending, the finish, the conclusion that awaits every believer—death has been destroyed. This is the conclusion that every believer can count upon—death is not the end for us.

You Must Believe in the Saint's Reward

The third thing on Paul's must-believe list was to believe in the **saint's reward**. Bruce Larson once wrote, "The events of the resurrection cannot be reduced to a creed or to a philosophy. We are not asked to believe in the doctrine of the resurrection. We are asked to meet the person who was resurrected from the dead." The resurrection is not something in one's checklist of things about which one can say, "OK, I believe in that." One must experience the resurrection by having experienced the Lord Jesus in one's own life. And so the third thing to believe is that there is a saintly reward.

One shows commitment to this belief by making **right choices**. 1 Corinthians 15:32 says, "If I fought wild animals in Ephesus with only human hope, what good does that do me? If the dead are not raised, Let us eat and drink for tomorrow we die. Do not be deceived: Bad company corrupts good morals, become right minded and stop sinning, because some people are ignorant about God. I say this to your shame." The world's philosophy posited, "Eat, drink for tomorrow we die." In classical literature, Herodotus, a Greek historian, told about an Egyptian custom that at parties and banquets a servant would carry around a two-foot wooden box. Inside the box would be a little wooden doll. The servant would tell all the guests at festive occasions "drink and be merry, for when you die such will be you." Isn't that a great icebreaker?

Jesus told a parable about a rich man who spent his entire life accumulating possessions. His philosophy of life is found in the parable in Luke 12:19, "And then I'll say to myself, 'You have many goods stored up for many years. Take it easy; eat, drink and enjoy yourself.'" Our culture tries to suck us into believing this philosophy. What did Paul say? "Become right-minded. Make good choices" (1 Cor. 15:34).

It is easy to become enamored with the world's way of "eat and drink, for tomorrow we die." But Paul said to be committed to right choices. When we are committed to right choices, we are also committed to **reject corruption**: "So it is with the resurrection of the dead: Sown in corruption, raised in incorruption" (1 Cor. 15:42). What does it mean to be "raised in incorruption?" "Sown in corruption" was Paul's way of referring to death. The next two verses give several illustrative comparisons to aid in our interpretation. "Sown in dishonor, raised in glory; sown in weakness, raised in power; sown a natural body, raised a spiritual body" (1 Cor. 15:43).

In the phrase, "sown in dishonor," the word "dishonor" means lacking attractiveness. I have never thought anyone looked attractive as a corpse. The most complimentary thing that any one has ever said about a loved one after death is that he or she looked natural or peaceful. No one says that a dead person looks attractive, because death is not attractive. The word "dishonor" can also mean humiliation. Have you ever said, "I don't want anyone to see me like this?" Perhaps you have made a decision that when death comes, you want a closed casket at your funeral.

We are sown in dishonor but "raised in glory," because glory describes our heavenly bodies. Glory describes what our bodies will be like after resurrection. I may not want anyone to see me like this before I receive a resurrected body, but I want everyone to see me after I have been made eternal. I want everyone to see my glorified body. My glorified body is going to be able to run like I have never been able to run before, breathe like I have never been able to breath before, jump like I've never been able to jump before. We are "sown in dishonor, raised in glory." I do not buy for a moment the world's philosophy that says "born to die." I am not buying for a moment that life in only about the "here and now." Because I was born to live in a relationship with God, I make my choices and reject the corruption of this world.

Paul was committed to right choices; part of making those right choices was exercising one's commitment to reject corruption. Ultimately Paul was committed to **real change**. We need a change. 1 Corinthians 15: 50 says, "Brothers, I tell you this flesh and blood cannot inherit the Kingdom of God, and corruption cannot inherit incorruption. Listen I am telling you a mystery. We will not all fall asleep, but we will all be changed." President Barak Obama got elected with the slogan "Change we can believe in." Long before him, Paul proclaimed, "This is the kind of change that I can believe in."

Job is considered the oldest recorded book in the Bible. It's the oldest writing that we have and has the most timeless theme. Job 14:14 asks, "When a man dies will he come back to life? If so, I would wait all the days of my struggle until my relief (change) has come." Job was asking the most important question that anyone can ask when a person died: "Is there any such thing as life after death?" Job had come to the conclusion that the only way there could possibly be life beyond this life was through a change. Without a change, one's heart could not beat endlessly, one's brain would not function continuously, and one's lungs would not expand and contract effortlessly.

Job came to some really serious conclusions about where and how that change could take place. In Job 19:25 Job said, "I know my living Redeemer and He will stand on the dust at last. Even after my skin has been destroyed, yet I will see God in my flesh. I will see myself; my eyes will look at Him, and not as a stranger. My heart longs within me." This was written thousands of years prior to the birth of Jesus Christ! But Job revealed the only way that anyone can know he or she has life beyond this life. There must be a redeemer who will stand upon the earth in the last days; He is the one who is going to take one's body and allow one to live with God forever. Paul said, in effect, "Job, you are right." In 1 Corinthians15:54-57, Paul said, "Death has been swallowed up in victory. O Death where is your victory? O Death, where is your sting? Now the sting of Death is sin, and the power of sin is the law. But thanks be to God, who gives us the victory through our Lord Jesus Christ!" There is a redeemer. There is one who can take you to heaven, one who will stand upon the earth in the last days and can redeem your body, claiming it from the grave.

Paul summarized his message in 1 Corinthians 15: 58, "Therefore, my dear brothers, be steadfast, immovable, always excelling in the Lord's work, knowing that your labor in the Lord is not in vain." As I read this verse, it reminds me of one of my favorite television commercials. During the winter season, a man leaves his office to find his car covered in ice and snow. He begins the laborious task of cleaning his car of the ice covering. During his painstaking task he falls in the frozen mess. Finally, completed the frigid job, the man pushes the button to his automatic door locks and with despair watches the lights flash to the car next to the one he has just cleaned. This guy's labor has been in vain.

I want to save you that experience. No matter how hard you try, no matter how cleaned up you think you have made your life, no matter how much you have done, your labor is in vain without believing in the resurrection. Once more, Romans 10:9-10 helps us grasp this point: "If you confess with your mouth, 'Jesus is Lord,' and believe in your heart that God has raised Him from the dead, you will be saved. With the heart one believes, resulting in righteousness, and with the mouth confesses, resulting in salvation." Salvation is not measured on the scales of good and evil, where if one has more good than evil on one's side, then one receives a heavenly reward. The Bible teaches that our labor is in vain unless we receive the reality of the resurrection into your lives. You can work as hard as you want and you can do as many good—even great—things as you want, you can give your life to great causes, but until the reality of Jesus Christ has enveloped your life, your labor is in vain. Don't labor in vain. You must believe.

LESSON 12:
MANAGE YOUR
LIFE

Paul moved his letter's message from an emphasis on theology in Chapter 15 to a very practical lesson of advice in Chapter 16. He said one needed a balance between doctrine and duty, between worship and work. Christianity is not just a belief system. It is not just checking off a list of what one believes, it is a system of behavior. It describes what one actually does in life. So how does one manage life? Earlier in 1 Corinthians 4, Paul referred to Christians as "managers." He said," A person should consider us in this way as servants of Christ and managers of God's mysteries. In this regard it is expected of managers that each one be found faithful" (1 Cor. 4:1-2).

I often hear people lament, "Pastor, I believe, but my life is spinning out of control." Newsweek ran an article in 2001 about one family's hectic schedule.[1] The magazine introduced us to a Christian mom named Kim Lawrence, 42 years old, mother of three boys, and head of the math department at John Cooper School in The Woodlands, Texas. The article detailed a day in the life of this typical American household. Kim, a Christian schoolteacher, reported this schedule: 5:00 a.m., wake up; 5:15 a.m.–6:50 a.m., prepare breakfast, wake up my boys, shower, and get ready for work; 6:20 a.m., husband, Jerry, drops off David for basketball practice on his way to work; 6:50 a.m., drive Jonathan to school and backtrack to school for Jackson, which is where I work; 7:35 a.m., walk Jackson to class; 7:45 a.m.–5:00 p.m., teaching, tutoring, and study hall with a quick diet drink for lunch; 5:00 p.m., commute home; 5:30 p.m.–7:30 p.m., homework, laundry, prepare dinner; 6:00 p.m., some evenings Jerry takes Jackson to soccer or Jonathan to youth group at church; 7:30 p.m., dinner; 7:50 p.m.–10:00 p.m., help with homework, projects, vocabulary words, research papers, and Internet searches; 10:00 p.m.–11:00 p.m., grade papers, make lesson plans for tomorrow; 11:00 p.m., bed; and then, in exasperation, start again in six hours.

Unfortunately, I sense that many of the readers of this book could rehearse a similar day in their recent past. It is not your belief system that is called into question. The fact that you are reading this book indicates something about your belief. But, when it comes to management of life, you are seeking wisdom and advice. What follows is Paul's teaching to the Corinthians about managing life.

Manage Your Money

In this closing chapter, Paul turned to the practical and gave management advice in three critical areas of life. The first piece of advice he covered was **manage your money well**. Often we refer to this as stewardship, a biblical word. The word *steward* simply means *manager*. It connotes the idea that God owns everything. All things belong to him. He allows us the opportunity to manage it while we are here.

Elmer Towns, the co-founder of Liberty University, teaches a pastors' class at the Thomas Road Baptist Church, Lynchburg, Virginia. His most requested lesson is one he entitles "Who Owns Your French Fries?"[2] It is the story of a man who buys his little boy some French fries at McDonald's. The father does what all fathers do; he reaches over and takes one of the fries on the way home to taste it. The boy slaps his dad's hand and says, "Don't touch my French fries." The father thinks to himself, "My son is acting in selfishness." The father knows that he has bought the French fries and they truly belong to him. The father also knows that the son belongs to him. The father could get angry and never buy his son another French fry or he could teach his son a lesson and bury his son in French fries. But the aggrieved father asks, "Why is my son so selfish? I've given him a whole package of fries and I am only taking this one."

In that same vein, God has provided us everything in our lives. When he asks something from us, for example a tithe to his church, people figuratively slap his hand and say, "Keep your hands off my money." Do we not know that God owns everything we have? He wants us to manage things for his glory. God expects us to manage our time, our talent, our temple, our testimony, and our treasure according to his Word.

Who owns your French fries? Paul, in the beginning of 1 Corinthians 16, gave five very basic principles of handling church finances.

> Now about the collection for the saints: you should do the same as I instructed the Galatian churches. On the first day of the week, each of you is to set something aside and save to the extent that he prospers, so that no collection will need to be made when I come. And when I arrive, I will send those whom you recommend by letter to carry your gracious gift to Jerusalem. If it is also suitable for me to go, they will travel with me (1 Cor. 16:1-4).

First, this is **purposeful giving**. Paul said this collection was for the saints. People needed to know that when they gave to a ministry, that real ministry was being accomplished. This particular offering was a relief offering. It was for the poor in Jerusalem, but its purpose was not just to meet the needs of impoverished people. There were other underlying purposes. When the offering was collected, it **demonstrated unity**. It was a way to build bridges. I believe the collective way we support missions, called the Cooperative Program, has made Southern Baptists the fastest growing evangelical denomination in the world. The Cooperative Program allows small churches and megachurches alike to aid in keeping 5,200 international missionaries and nearly 5,000 at North American missionaries involved in ministry. The Corinthians' offering was a demonstration of unity. It was also a **demonstration of Christianity**. Great brotherhoods in that time were established to help the poor, much like civic and community organizations do today. To me, it is shameful when a civic organization does more than does the church to care for the world. Giving declares to a community that we care!

The offering allowed the early church a **demonstration of charity**. Often I ask people, "If you had a million dollars, what would you do with it? If you wish you had a million dollars and God were to grant that wish, what would you do with it?" The first answer often is a reflection of self rather than how one would invest it or give it away. Could it be that is why God never provides some of those things in our lives, because we have never gotten past the tendency to lavish the blessings upon ourselves?

The Corinthians gave purposefully a collection for the saints. The Corinthians giving was also **planned giving**. Paul said, "On the first day of the week." Sunday had become the accepted day of worship by this time and giving was intended to be a part of Christian worship. Acts 20:7 states, "On the first day of the week, we assembled to break bread. Paul spoke to them, and since he was about to depart the next day, he extended his message until midnight." The first day of the week was set aside for worship; a part of worship was giving. The lesson for us is that giving should be systematic and is unmistakably linked to our relationship with God.

The Corinthian offering was purposeful giving, planned giving, and also **personal giving**. Paul commissioned each member of the church in Corinth. Paul wanted every one of them to enjoy the blessings of giving. God had a blessing for those who give. In Malachi 3:8, Malachi, the prophet, proclaimed that a non-giving believer is actually a thief. Malachi proclaimed, "Will a man rob God? Yet are robbing Me! You ask: 'How do we rob you?' By not making the payments, of 10 percent into the storehouse."

We have experienced some thefts around our church in the past year. This has been a little disturbing. We had a break-in of our tool shed and some of our power tools were taken. These are things that people easily could use or sell. Some video equipment was stolen this past year. But the most disturbing crime occurred in the summer when people tore into our air-conditioning units in order to steal the copper tubing. I had no idea that there was such a market for copper tubing that people would break into air conditioners. In leadership sessions people ask, "Why would people steal from the church?" It is far more disturbing than a person stealing from the church when the collection plate is passed and people rob from God by not giving.

Another aspect of the Corinthian offering was that it displayed **proportionate giving**. Paul said, "To the extent that He prospers you." Have you ever thought that God gave the concept of the tithe to be a minimum threshold about which people could say, "That is where we start!"? It is an accepted practice in restaurants to tip your server; a typical tip was once 15 percent or so. Today a more acceptable practice is about 18 percent or even 20 percent. People want to know what is typical. You want to do the right thing.

My wife, Glenda, and I enjoy going to the dinner theatre. We have debated about what is the proper tip for dinner theatre because not all of one's cost is restaurant-related. There is a food and service portion and an entertainment portion. At the Dinner Theatre we attend they have begun to print in the program a tipping guide to what would be appropriate.

There was a question of appropriateness for the church in Corinth. Paul said that if one wanted to know the answer of appropriateness, look at what the Bible teaches, what has been true since the Old Testament. People come to me and say, "But Pastor, that's Old Testament law." Many people say dismiss passage as Old Testament law because they don't want to do anything. Some people tell me, "Pastor, I can't afford to tithe." As the saying has it, when your outgo exceeds your income, then your upkeep is going to be your downfall. An open heart can't have a closed fist.

Finally, the Corinthian offering was **protected giving**. In 1 Corinthians 16:3-4, Paul pointed out that he wanted the offering to be handled above board and that there was a careful plan protecting these gifts as they were being transported from one location to the other. Paul said, "Those who will go with me whom you recommend by letter." Paul wanted this offering to be seen through eyes of integrity and honesty. Later in 2 Corinthians 8:20-21, he said, "We are taking this precaution so that no one can find fault with us concerning the large sum administered by us. For we are making provision for what is honorable, not only before the Lord but also before men." We learn that everything should be above board and done with honesty and integrity; we are called to manager our money well.

Manage Your Ministry

The second area about which Paul gave advice was **management of one's ministry**. When it came to ministry, Paul saw opportunities, opposition, and obligations. **During times of opportunity, be fruitful**, he advised. In 1 Corinthians 16:5-9, Paul shared a brief itinerary of his upcoming travels and ministry. He closed with these words, "A wide door for effective ministry has been opened to me." An opportunity had arisen to do some effective ministry. In Ephesians 5:15-16, Paul wrote, "Be careful then how you live, not as unwise but as wise; making the most of every opportunity because the days are evil" (NIV). Everyone has probably missed opportunities in one's life. Or maybe one has heard testimonies of missed opportunities.

Thomas Watson was the chairman of IBM in 1943. He made the statement, "I think there is a world for maybe five computers." Realizing that was 1943, fast forward to 1957 when the editor of business text books for Prentice Hall said, "I've traveled the length and the width of this country, talked with the best people, and I can assure you that data processing is a fad and will not last the year." Jump another two decades to 1977, when Ken Olsen, president and founder of Digital Equipment Corporation said, "There is no reason anyone would ever want a computer in their home." But there was one magazine that relentlessly predicted the rise of technology, *Popular Mechanics*. In 1949, it claimed, "Computers in the future may weigh as little as one and a half tons.... However, the needed technology will be economically impossible for the average home."[3] When you have an opportunity, let your actions be fruitful.

I served as a pastor in Tennessee for thirteen years and during my tenure in Tennessee our church conducted a stewardship campaign in which we asked members of the church to give stewardship testimonies. One gentleman, asked to give a testimony, stood to speak to the congregation. I did not know the particulars of what he was about to share. He began, "I was thrilled to be given this opportunity to share with you about stewardship in my life. Many of you may know that I had the opportunity as a very young man to invest in a tract of land in the rural section of my home county. Local businessmen asked me to become a partner in their development plan. I passed on that opportunity. That rural section of my home county is now known as Pigeon Forge, Tennessee, and the Gateway to the Smoky Mountains. A few years later some a local radio station owner asked me to back and invest in a young singer who played the drums for the county high school marching band. I met with the backwoods and bashful young lady and didn't see much future for her so I passed on the opportunity. Many of you may know the young lady; her name is Dolly Parton." I thought to myself, this is the sorriest stewardship testimony I have ever heard! But then the testimony concluded, "But then two men came to our home and provided me an opportunity to exchange my sin for the life of Christ, to invest my life in an eternal project that would have everlasting reward. I may have missed big opportunities in my young life, but I seized the greatest opportunity and I have never regretted it." When opportunities abound, act to be fruitful.

The second aspect of managing one's ministry is remembering that **during opposition, be firm.** At the end of 1 Corinthians 16:9, Paul said, "Yet many opposed me." Paul was neither a pessimist nor an optimist; Paul was a realist. He knew that whenever one ministers in the name of Christ, one would suffer opposition. Paul said to Timothy, "All who live godly in Christ Jesus will suffer persecution" (in 2 Tim. 3:12). That is a viable promise. Not many people write down that verse in the file leafs of their Bible. "All who live godly in Christ Jesus will suffer persecution." That is a promise; you can rely upon it, you can count on it.

Dr. John White, a professor of psychiatry for years, who has gone to be with the Lord, wrote a classic devotional back in the 1970s entitled, *The Fight: A Practical Handbook to Christian Living.* In his book, White said, "If you play it cool and decide not to be a fanatic about your Christianity, you will have no trouble from them (meaning the world) but if you are serious about Christ being your Lord and your God, you can expect opposition."[4]

David Livingston was one of the pioneer missionaries to Africa. He walked nearly 29,000 miles during his lifetime. His wife died very early in his ministry. He faced stiff opposition from Scottish brethren back home and ministered the latter half of his life despite partial blindness. Livingston had a common prayer written in his journal. It said, "Send me anywhere, only go with me; lay any burden on me, only sustain me; sever me from any tie but the tie that binds me to your service and to your heart."[5] Dr. Joseph Stowell, past President of Moody Bible Institute commented, "I repeat this prayer every morning. It reminds us that during times of opposition, we need to stand firm.

A third aspect of managing one's ministry entails remembering that **during times of obligation, be faithful**. In 1 Corinthians 16:10, Paul said, "If Timothy comes, see that he has nothing to fear from you, because he is doing the Lord's work, just as I am." Why would Timothy have anything to fear from the Corinthians? The only reason that Timothy would be fearful was that they were expecting Paul, but Timothy arrived instead. If one were expecting Billy Graham and I came instead, some of you would be extremely disappointed. In fact, most of you would be extremely disappointed. Paul said in essence, "You may have been expecting me, but Timothy is coming; respect him." Why respect him? Not because he is a scholar, nor because he is an excellent pulpiteer, not because he will have all the answers for you; no, one should respect him because he is doing the work of the Lord. Sometimes there is no other reason to be supportive and encouraging beyond knowing God is doing his work.

Manage Your Manners

Paul's concluding advice to the Corinthians was to **manage their manners**. He gave three closing words about how Christians ought to act in everyday life. Paul challenged believers to have **strong attributes**. In 1 Corinthians 16:13 he wrote, "Be alert, stand firm in the faith, be brave and strong." There are four imperatives in this one verse. An imperative in the Greek language is a commandment. It is like a general giving a command to his army, to his troops. Paul commanded, "Be alert, stand firm, be brave, and be strong." The word "brave" in the King James Version is translated "quit you like men." That is an unusual phrase…"quit you like men." It is a phrase that literally means to act like a man, act grown up. Have strong attributes, be brave and be strong.

In the nineteenth century, lighthouses dotted the coastline of the United States. Before the days of modern technology, the lighthouse keeper was considered the most valuable person in a coastal community. These men and their entire families would live either in the lighthouse or right next to it. And if the lighthouse captain were to take ill, a family member was commissioned to take over immediately. Such was the case of Hosea Lewis, who, in 1853, became the lighthouse captain of the Lime Rock Island lighthouse in Newport, Rhode Island. Four years later, Lewis suffered a stroke. His wife had already died, so his teenage daughter, Ida, assumed the responsibility of the lighthouse. Daily, Ida would make sure her siblings were taken to school, which involved a 500-yard rowboat ride to the main land. But this teenager gained prominence and fame when, at the age of sixteen, she rescued four men from a capsized boat. On March 29, 1869, Ida saved two other drowning service men near Fort Adams. She gained such notoriety that President Ulysses S. Grant came to visit her in Newport. Later that year, Ida rescued an additional two soldiers. All told, Ida Lewis personally saved about twenty-five people in more than fifty years of being the lighthouse keeper. She was last reported to have rescued someone when she was sixty-three years old—a friend who was on her way to the lighthouse to visit Ida. Asked where she found strength and courage for such a feat, Ida said, "I don't know, I ain't particularly strong, the Lord almighty give it to me when I need it and that's all I know."[6]

Paul challenged the Corinthians to have not only strong attributes, but also a **servant's action**. 1 Corinthians 16:15-18 states, "Brothers, you know the household of Stephanas: they are the first fruits of Achaia and have devoted themselves to serving the saints, I urge you also to submit to such people." Paul picked a role model family from their peers and said what he wanted his readers to know about them. First of all, they were self-appointed servants. They had devoted themselves to serving the saints. In one translation it says they were "addicted" to the service of the saints. I love that phrase. Can you imagine people who are addicted to ministry? In 1 Corinthians 16:16-17, Paul wrote that they were leaders, while still laborers. And in the next verse, Paul described this family as an answer to the prayers of its pastor. 1 Peter 4:10 states, "Based on the gift that they have received, everyone should use it to serve others, as good managers of the varied grace of God."

A good manger is one who has strong attributes. A good manager is someone who displays servant actions in their life. Finally, a good manager is someone who has **sincere acceptance**. When Paul arrived at the conclusion of his letter and was signing it, he wrote, "My love be with all of you in Christ Jesus" (1 Cor. 16:24). Some people think this is one of the first indicators Paul was a "Southern" Baptist or at least a southerner, because he said, "I love you all!" Paul meant it, saying, basically, "Followers of Cephas and followers of Apollos who had divided the church into segments, I love all of you. Young men who had disgraced the church by your morally outrageous behavior, I love all of you! Disruptive church members who are arguing over which of the spiritual gifts you have, I love all of you!"

Business Week recently ran an article on Management Fears. The writer asked managers across the United States which of their work-related activities made them the most uncomfortable. The number-one response, from 73 percent, said, "Building relationships with people I don't like. Because I know that in order for my business to be functional, I have to build relationships with people and work with people that I am not sure I even like."[7] Paul concluded this great letter by saying, "I love all of you. I have learned that, regardless of division, I love all of you."

On April 20, 2009, about 22,000 people lined up in the streets of Boston, Massachusetts, to run the world's oldest annual road race event, the Boston Marathon. This race covers 26 miles, 385 yards. One must have won a sanctioned marathon or had a qualifying time in a sanctioned marathon to even enter the race. Many people will collapse right after they finish this race. Some will not even make it to the finish line. Of the 22,000 participants, in reality, only a handful has any chance of winning the race. Why run this grueling race? The reward lies in the run. The reward is in just having the opportunity to be in it. The reward comes in saying, "I ran in the Boston Marathon." Maybe you will never gain national notoriety or ever be on the front page of a newspaper, but the reward comes from participating, being someone who ran the race and ran it well. Paul told the church at Corinth, it is not about playing church, it is not about avoiding church, it is not about doing church, it is not about growing the church, it is about **being the church**. It is realizing where you are and what God has for you in your life. Ultimately, it is about being the church that God intended for you to be.

EPILOGUE

While writing this book, I attended church every week. I affirm that gathering together for worship is a mandate for all believers (Hebrews 10:25). The church gathers so that we may be effective when the church scatters. Church attendance should not be seen as merely a good suggestion, but rather the entry point to genuinely "being the church." However, the lesson of being the church is seldom learned beneath the steeple of the church facility.

Recently my wife, Glenda, had surgery. During her time of convalescence at home, church family members sprang into action to minister to us. Our small group coordinated meals to be delivered to our home for the first two weeks. Other church members stopped by to check on her and offered to perform tasks from running errands to cleaning our house. Why were these people doing these things? No one asked them to perform these duties. They were "being the church."

One of my favorite New Testaments stories is about Jesus, weary from teaching the multitudes, who gets into a boat with his disciples to get away from the crowds (Mark 4:35-41). Jesus needs some rest and relaxation. He is so fatigued that he immediately falls asleep in the boat. While he is resting, a nasty storm appears on the horizon and the disciples begin to panic. The same men who had just witnessed Jesus feed 5,000 people with the provision of a little boy's lunch are now acting like faithless cowards trembling in fear of a storm. One can criticize someone else's fears, but that doesn't take away the reality of the fear to them. The disciples awaken Jesus from his needed rest and ask, "Do you care that we are going to die?" Jesus does not scold the disciples, nor does he defend the fact that he cares intimately about them. He walks to the edge of the boat, rebukes the storm, and immediately the chaotic situation is brought under control. Jesus did not say that he cared. He showed that he cared. The world is not interested in hearing how much the church cares about them. But the world desperately desires to see the caring hands of the church.

Easter Sunday is a time when marginally involved church members and attendees reappear in a worship service. Churches across America and around the world are filled to capacity with ladies in new hats and men sporting new ties. This past Easter, we challenged our church family to seize this opportunity to invite friend or family members who are not believers to attend with them. We developed a prayer list of over 100 names of "people in process" who were invitees to our Easter services. This list is the beginning of "being the church." To be the church we must show that we care and be willing to share. Invest in someone's life. Tell them the difference that Christ has made in you. Go forth and **be the church!**

INTRODUCTION

1 Focus on the Family's "Pastor's Weekly Briefing," February 19, 2005 (Access http://www.parsonage.org/pwb).
2 http://sermoncental.com
3 http://mygoal.com/newyears.html

LESSON ONE

1 Adrian Rogers, *Mastering Your Emotions* (Nashville, TN: Broadman Press, 1988).

LESSON TWO

1 http://www.businessknowledgesource.com/smallbusiness/how_to_unify_employees_for_an_effective_team_026127.html
2 Richard J. Foster, *Streams of Living Water* (New York: Harper Collins, 1988).

LESSON THREE

1 http://www.christianitytoday.com/yc (June 7, 2003).
2 Reggie McNeal, *The Present Future* (San Francisco, CA: Josey Bass, 2003).

3 http://www.barna.org-update/article/5-barna-update/63-how-americas-faith-has-changed-since-9-11.
4 Terry Teykl, *Blueprints for the House of Prayer* (Spring, TX: Prayer Point Press, 1997), p. 22.
5 http://sermoncentral.com
6 Warren Wiersbe, *Be Wise* (Wheaton, IL: Victor Books, 1985).
7 Randy Frazee, *The Connecting Church* (Grand Rapids, MI: Zondervan, 2001), pp. 52-53.

LESSON FOUR

1 " Indianapolis Star," (November 5, 2008).
2 "Focal Point" is a free weekly bible email from *Focus Magazine* (quoted summer, 2009, p.19).
3 http://barna.org (May 6, 2003 Barna Update).
4 http://sermoncental.com
5 "Family Circle Magazine" (June, 2003), as reported in Focus on the Family's " Pastor's Weekly Update".

LESSON FIVE

1 http://sermoncentral.com
2 Steve McVey, *Grace Walk* (Eugene, OR: Harvest House Publishers, 1995).

LESSON SIX

1 http://www.onenewsnow.com (January 8, 2007).
2 U.S. Census estimates quoted in "USA Today" (September 12, 2007).
3 http://sermoncentral.com
4 http://www.onenewsnow.com
5 http://lifeway.com/lwc
6 http://barna.org (January, 2000).
7 http://sermoncentral.com
8 http://onenewsnow.com (January 8, 2007).

9 Adrian Rogers, *Ten Secrets For a Successful Family* (Wheaton, IL: Crossway Books, 1996), pp.122-123.

10 As reported by "The Foster Network" (October 7, 1999).

11 Charles Colson, Nancy Pearcy, *How Now Shall We Live* (Chicago, IL: Tyndale House Publishers, 2004).

12 Charles Swindoll, *The Quest for Character*, (Grand Rapids, MI: Zondervan, 1993).

LESSON SEVEN

1 http://sermoncentral.com
2 http://journal.sjdm.org/
3 John Maxwell, *21 Irrefutable Laws of Leadership* (Nashville, TN: Thomas Nelson, 2007).

LESSON EIGHT

1 http://sermoncentral.com
2 Charles Swindoll, *Living on the Ragged Edge*, (Nashville, TN: Thomas Nelson, 1990).
3 http://sermoncental.com
4 "Loose Change Newsletter," (Nov- Dec, 1995).
5 K.P.Yohnnon, *Revolution in World Missions* (Carrolton, TX: Gospel for Asia Books), pp.39-40.
6 William Hendricks, *Exit Interviews: Revealing Stories of Why People are Leaving Church* (Chicago, IL: Moody Press, 1993).

LESSON NINE

1 *The Best of Harvard Business Review* (Boston, MA: Harvard Business School Press, 1999).
2 http://www.marcusbuckingham.com
3 http://sermoncentral.com
4 http://www.sermonillustrations.com/a-z/t/talent.htm
5 http://sermoncentral.com

LESSON TEN

1 www.brainyquote.com/quote/aithors/j/jothan_swift_4.html'
2 Luther Joe Thompson, *Love is Alive* (Nashville, TN: Broadman and Holman Publishers, 1980).
3 http:/Fathergilles.net/inspirations/st_valentine_legend

LESSON ELEVEN

1 http://www.thetruthproject.org/
2 AP article quoted in "Indianapolis Star," (March 9, 2009).
3 AP article quoted in "Indianapolis Star," (March 10, 2009).
4 James Emory White, *Rethinking the Church* (Grand Rapids, MI: Baker Books, 1997).
5 http://sermoncentral.com/articleb.asp?article=Easter-Illustrations-PowerPoints and elsewhere.

LESSON TWELVE

1 "Newsweek Magazine," (January 29, 2001), p.50.
2 http://sermoncentral.com
3 Ibid.
4 John White, *The Fight: A Practical Handbook for Christian Living*, (Downers Grove, IL: Intervarsity Press, 1976).
5 Joseph Stowell, *Through the Fire* (Wheaton, IL: Victor Books, 1985), p.150.
6 http://www.vais.net~cypress/ida.htm
7 "Business Week Magazine," (July 7, 2003).

ABOUT THE AUTHOR

Dr. Mark Hearn is pastor of Northside Baptist Church, the largest Southern Baptist church in Indianapolis. He has served as senior pastor in Southern Baptist churches for 28 years. Mark has taught as adjunct professor of Evangelism and Discipleship at both Crossroads Bible College in Indianapolis and Oklahoma Baptist University. He is past president of the State Convention of Baptists in Indiana and past first vice president of the Georgia Baptist Convention. He was named to the "Hall of Fame" (Distinguished Alumni) of Pulaski County High School in Pulaski, Virginia. Mark is a graduate of Carson–Newman College (BA), Southern Baptist Theological Seminary (M. Div.) and Luther Rice Seminary (D. Min.). He and his wife, Glenda, have four grown daughters and three grandsons.

LaVergne, TN USA
12 July 2010
189238LV00004B/81/P